Sanctified Weakness

Sanctified Weakness

Jeremy V Fletcher

Editor: Albert A C Waite, PhD

MANDRA PUBLISHING

First published in 2002 by
Mandra Publishing
P.O. Box 5136
Riseley
RG7 1GT

ISBN 0-9540429-2-1

British Library Cataloguing in Publication Data.
A catalogue record for this book is available from the British Library.

Printed and bound in Great Britain by
Bookcraft
Midsomer Norton
Bath, BA3 4BS

This book is dedicated to Maizie and Victor Fletcher - parents

BENEFICIARIES

All the profit from the sale of this book will benefit:

The Sickle Cell Society, 54 Station Road, London, NW10 4UA

Comment: The Sickle Cell Society is grateful that the Fletcher family acknowledges our efforts by inviting our endorsement of this initiative in memory of Jeremy.

Dr. asa'ah Nkohkwo FRSH
Director of the Society
October 2002

and

The development programme of Palmer's Cross SDA Church, Maypen, Jamaica

COMMENTS

This book will enthuse both young and old to love, honour and worship our amazing Lord. Jeremy was able to bring the Bible to life in a manner that only he could and keep the attention of all who listened and wanted to hear. He had skills, insight and experience beyond his years and for those of us who knew him, personally, the contents of the book will always enable us to visualise and hear a young man with a very special gift from God. I know that it will inspire all who delve into its pages.

I particularly like chapter 2, 'Dream On'. He preached this message at the Stanborough Secondary School Day of Fellowship, where he challenged the students to do great things, with God in charge of their plans. When he made the altar call, my son, aged 10, made his decision for Christ that day. Unfortunately, Jeremy did not live to see him baptised the following May. I will always be grateful to God for the influence this messenger from God brought to my son.
Lydia Dean

The greatest influence that came from our friendship was the joint and yet personal desire to work for God and to preach the gospel.... The impact of Jeremy's life was all the impetus needed to bring people from all walks of life together, where nothing else seemingly would.
Olsen Roberts

Sanctified Weakness, is an intriguing mixture of sermons. They are truly inspiring, full of hope and encouragement, reaching out to young people at their level.

The reader will discover how Jeremy shares his experiences from across the spectrum of life: emotionally, spiritually and secularly and how his heart sang of his love for his Lord, despite trials and obstacles, and yet with no apology or embarrassment.

The chapters are short, enabling the reader to stay focused. They were crafted not just for delivery and enjoyment, but also to point the way to God, through Jesus, our Saviour. All chapters have a personal element in them. For me, the most poignant is the final one: *"Lord, if You Had Been Here...."*

I'm blessed to have known Jeremy, albeit very briefly. Nevertheless, if I hadn't met him, having read *Sanctified Weakness*, I certainly know in Whom he truly believed. You will be blessed too.
Jacquelyn Johnson

This book is substantive in its Biblical content. It is inspiring, motivating and challenging in its language. *Sanctified Weakness* should be read by all our young people, Pastors and those who preach. It could be a catalyst for the standard of sermons that need to be preached in these uncertain times.
Pastor Steve Palmer (Youth Director)

ABOUT THE AUTHOR

Jeremy Victor Fletcher BA, BA

(See appendix one)

ACKNOWLEDGEMENTS

Thank you to the many individuals who heard Jeremy preach and said, "Yes, it would be good to have his work in print."

To Dr Patrick Herbert who added significantly to chapters four and five; Greg Wilson whose artistic skills shine through on the cover; Jacquelyn Johnson and Alicia A C Waite – for both contributing word processing and valuable editorial skills; Jackie Hines for typing some of the chapters, and Mandra Publishing for facilitating the publishing of this volume.

There are others who contributed significantly, including those who read the manuscript and provided helpful comments – all your contributions are sincerely acknowledged.

CONTENTS

FROM THE EDITOR

You, the reader, have something unique in your hand. *Sanctified Weakness* is much more than a collection of inspirational sermons, written in the language of young people. It is also the story of a life, weak in the flesh, but touched by God.

In editing Jeremy's sermons, which were not originally prepared for publication, my task was made easier, in that Jeremy was a manuscript preacher. I was compelled to stay with his style and idiosyncrasies, as this would maintain the originality that the material deserves. I am delighted that I imposed such discipline on myself and am confident you will appreciate the outcome.

While each chapter in the book is a special, I must draw your attention to the next section, where Pastor and Mrs Hall's letter (which I titled: Inspirational Guidance from Scotland) gives a classic synthesis of human weakness and scripture, to answer their own wandering – "what to say to you that would mean anything." This too, illuminates the title – *Sanctified Weakness*.

Another inspired addition, is the last section in the book, which was presented at Jeremy's funeral by his best friend, Olsen. I challenge you to read *What a tribute can never say* without it having an impact on you!

It is hoped that through the pages of this book, many more individuals, than those who heard Jeremy when he delivered the sermons in person, will also be challenged and inspired by the work of a young man, who brought the Bible to life, in a manner that only he could.

Every young Christian person, should own a copy of *Sanctified Weakness*. It offers a lifeline!

AACW
Conifers
October 2002

INSPIRATIONAL GUIDANCE FROM SCOTLAND

Dear Victor and Maizie

Since the sad, sad news reached us on Sabbath, that leaves you bereft of *both* your beloved sons, Chris and I have been thinking of you and praying for you and wondering what to say to you that would mean anything. Words seem such feeble things to bring any comfort in the dark distress that must hem you in on every side. Yet, in God's words, there is comfort for the sorest of hearts.

Jesus, our risen Lord, grieves with you for Jeremy and His love is deeper even than that of Mum and Dad. He called him to His service and he died in his Lord's service. The lengths of service isn't important; the service itself is all-important. John the Baptist prepared 30 years for just one year's work and then died a cruel and lonely death in Herod's dungeon. His work was complete. His grief-stricken, questioning followers sought comfort in coming to Jesus. And so may – indeed, so *must* we. There is nowhere else to go. And Jesus had nothing but words of high esteem for His herald.

My mind goes back to Job and his wife, who were prostate with grief when the most terrible news of all reached them on the heels of lowing all their possessions – the death of all their 10 sons and daughters. We can understand the bitterness and anger of Job's wife when later, in addition to their tremendous loss, she saw her husband in terrible pain and cried out, "Curse God and die."

Neither Job nor his wife even knew the cause of their sufferings – Satan's hatred of God. The agonised questions that press in upon us in our darkest hours, "Why…? Why me…? Why now?" were never answered for Job and his wife back then. The amazing thing about their story is they emerged from it stronger in faith with a deeper, more humble view of the wonderful character of God than ever before. It was a miracle of grace that they were enabled to look, not backward for the *cause* of their troubles, but forward to the *outcome* of their troubles.

I am sure that this seems impossible for you, so soon after suffering such a heavy blow, to grasp or experience. But the same grace that brought Job and his wife through the dark valley into the sunny uplands of trust and peace, will bring your through too.

Unburden your hearts in prayer. Whatever your present feelings may be – perplexity, anger, despair, numbness, rebellion even – try not to bottle the up, but be honest about them to your heavenly Father. They may seem to be things you don't wish to say, that perhaps you feel ought not to be said: but they are the truth about you, which our Saviour already knows and can do something about as soon as we open our hearts to Him and trust Him with our inmost thoughts. (The prayers of Jeremiah, e.g. 20:7-18, - notice the up and down of Jeremiah's mind in his distress, - and many of the Psalms show how open and unrestrained these godly men were in their hard times when talking to God.)

And if even this seems too much for you at present, can you alert a small circle of friends to come round and offer prayer for you? Jesus Himself presents all our awkward and stammering requests in His own language to His Father, fragrant with the incense of His own perfection. The angels are hovering around you, ready to perform the slightest service that will help you in this present time of need.

We remember you in the happier days, twenty years ago now.

They are good memories and are a blessing on the road as we make our way – rather more slowly these days – to the kingdom. When Jesus comes *it will all come right*, Victor and Maizie, and we shall rejoice for even in what our Lord has made of our lives.

Your friends in the love of Jesus,

Christine & Victor Hall
(Scotland, 1 August 2000)

Note: Used by kind permission of Christine Hall. Pastor Victor Hall died in 2001

1

CHASING BUBBLES

On 6 September 1997, millions of people unwittingly kept the Saturday Sabbath. Businesses of all descriptions were closed down, all over the country. Business meetings were cancelled, flights were rescheduled, as millions of people made their way to London, and over 2 billion others around the world stopped to watch on television. Not because the world had suddenly become Jews or Seventh-day Adventists, but rather this took place out of respect and, I might add, love for one woman.

The late Diana, Princess of Wales, a woman worshipped by billions - more than the Pope; a woman adored by billions - more than Michael Jackson; and a woman who was more widely held in higher esteem than the Queen herself.

Many have tried to identify the source of her appeal. On the day, in 1981, that Charles, Prince of Wales, married Lady Diana Spencer, the Archbishop of Canterbury expressed the feelings of the world when he declared, "Here is the stuff of which fairy tales are made." Yet that fairy tale ended, even before their divorce was announced.

'Newsweek' declared that she became adored for contradictory reasons, stating that the Princess of Wales was both a pop icon and the mother of kings. Emerging scathed from a disastrous marriage, Diana moved on and so did her public, loving her for her simplicity, tenderness and compassion. She had other causes to tend to – her sons, the sick, the dying, the war-ravaged and her own heart. For these reasons, she became the Queen of Hearts, the People's Princess, and, according to Tony Blair, "that's how she remains in our hearts and memories forever." But aside from all these descriptions of the source of Diana's appeal, there is one statement in 'Time' magazine, which significantly betrays the root cause of the fascination that she held for the world. It reads, "With her go the hopes of the world that had turned her life into part of its own projected biography, a fragile hope for a happy-ever-after, even in the face of adversity."

Let us pause to recognise that when the world struggled to come to terms with the death of a princess, it also struggled with the death of a dream. You see, the world was riveted when a seemingly ordinary woman was handed the dream on a plate, on the morning of 29th July 1981. The world was riveted to watch, as her ideal world came crashing down around her and all watched breathlessly. Each of her dreams vanished into nothingness, as life handed her a lemon every step of the way. It was rather like chasing bubbles, something that we used to do as children, finding that the moment we tried to catch it, it burst. Yet unwilling to learn from this experience, we went after the next bubble and after that burst, the next and the next and the next.

In fact, it seemed that we never got tired of chasing bubbles. We have since discovered that public interest played a part in Diana's untimely end. We may all recognise that the world, too, was busy chasing a bubble that burst, when the life of this princess was snuffed out. So, when I hear of the million floral tributes from places like China and other corners of the globe; when I hear of businesses shutting down on the most profitable shopping day; when I hear of the transport system overflowing with people travelling to see the proceedings, and an estimated 2.5 billion people, the biggest television audience in history, following along on their screens, I hear the world cry out, "How tragic!" How tragic to see life as a bubble, fragile and unstable! How tragic to have to pursue happiness and have it elude you! How tragic to be cut down in the prime of your life! After having achieved much of what one's heart desires, how tragic to have life itself taken away from her! How tragic to find that life, a life, any life is meaningless!

This is a conclusion that many have come to. Yet it is a misery that all have tasted at one time or another - the feeling that all your ventures have been foolish and futile, farcical and frustrating, without meaning and lacking purpose. It is almost as if you have been chasing a bubble that has burst and left you with nothing. The fact is that often in life we are drawn to things, seemingly important things, that require time and effort. We, willingly or not, put in this time and effort, only to find after a while that, whether successful or not, it has not been worthwhile.

All we seem to do in life is chase bubbles! Career bubbles, money bubbles, bubbles of independence, bubbles of respect, bubbles of romance, bubbles of pleasure, bubbles of knowledge through scholarly attainment and bubbles of perfection – all in the name of fulfilment. But guess what? It has all been done before. Mankind has not changed at all!

To state a 3000-year old phrase, "There is nothing new under the sun.... Vanity of vanities...says the preacher" (Ecclesiastes 1:2,9). "Meaningless, all is meaningless." Here is a man who tasted more misery than even the most dedicated of bubble chasers, because he had to try it all.

King Solomon of the mighty nation of Israel, the wisest and richest of all men, was cheered, feared and revered by men and women alike across the ancient world. This man had been there, seen it, done it and had the t-shirt to prove it. Yet, contrary to what one might think, he did not achieve nor realise his fragile hope for a happy-ever-after life through his exploits. In fact, his memoirs, Ecclesiastes, define what I have chosen to call 'bubble chasing' as meaningless and 'grasping for the wind'.

Collins defines *vanity* as, "the state or quality of being valueless or futile." The Hebrew word used for vanity here, is 'hebel', meaning breath, vapour or mist. Indeed, the semantics of this word illustrate Solomon's frustration of the futility of trying to grasp the wind. And he said that it was vanity, that the things he did were in vain. So what did Solomon do? Well, first he decided to increase his knowledge, so he studied not just to gain more knowledge, but to know more. That is, to be more clever than anyone had been before him. And he succeeded. But afterwards, he perceived it to be a grievous task given to a son of man – grasping for the wind. This led Solomon to say, "...in much wisdom is much grief. He that increases knowledge increases sorrow" (Ecclesiastes 1:18).

Next, he tried entertainment. In chapter 2, his verdict was that surely this also was vanity. "I said of laughter, it is madness and of pleasure, what does it accomplish?" (verse 2). You see, Solomon was just as foolish as we are, looking for happiness in the wrong places. So what did he do when despair and disillusionment set in? He turned to the bottle. He would drink wine for as long as the merest hint of sensibility allowed him to bring the cup to his lips. No solution there! So he began his search for perfection. The perfect palace, the perfect garden, the perfect household. He built for himself great pieces of architecture, beautiful gardens, water pools. He became a collector of rare and beautiful things - silver and gold, the treasures of kings. He became great and excelled all who were before him. In fact, everything you can think of to do, Solomon did in his own time and in his own way.

Solomon says, "whatever my eyes desired I did not keep from them. I did not withhold my heart from any pleasure" (verse 10). Now how many of us could say that? Solomon was also a great lover of women, setting a record which, I am sure, stands to this day - having no less than a thousand women, which means if he were to spend a day with each one it would take him a good three years to see them all. Seven hundred wives and three hundred mistresses, who lived up to the term for wife in Cockney colloquialism, "trouble and strife."

As you can imagine, there were bound to be problems of rivalry in a household of a thousand women, all sharing one man! One wonders, with three different texts in Proverbs dealing with the problem of a quarrelsome woman, if Solomon wrote them while he was still relatively single, or whether at the time he wrote them he knew more about it than he cared to let on. Proverbs 19:13 says, "A nagging wife is like water going drip-drip-drip." In Proverbs 21:9, it also says, "Better to live on the roof than share the house with a nagging wife." Proverbs 21:19 declares, "Better to live in the desert than with a nagging, complaining wife." Who knows what Solomon went through, except that the Bible says, "For it was so, when Solomon was old that his wives turned his heart after other gods" (1Kings 11:1-13). And Solomon found that rather than having more women to please him, he instead had more women to please.

In Ecclesiastes 2:17, Solomon says, "Therefore I hated life because all the work that was done under the sun was grievous to me, for all is meaningless and grasping for the wind." Generally, if you ask a person, "What do you want out of life?" Some will say, "To be comfortable"; some will say, "Someone or something to believe in"; some will say, " To find love and romance"; some will say, "To be independent"; and some will say, "To be my own boss." But we are all after the same thing. We are all struggling and striving for a fragile hope for a happy-ever-after life, even in the face of adversity. As people chase their bubbles they say to themselves, "If I can just get to the point where I fulfil this desire, then I will be happy. If I can just actualise my dream, my picture of perfection, then it will be enough. I don't want much, just this one thing and I'll be content." But you know what? We are all searching for the same thing - this utopian concept of the happy-ever-after feeling of ultimate fulfilment. And that is why we are chasing bubbles.

A lot of misery is associated with bubble-chasing. It can ruin your life in two ways. There is the pain of unrealised dreams. Also, on the other hand, there is the pain of realised dreams, when you discover that the dream you chased was not worthy of your life. People do not know what is missing in their lives; they only know that something is missing and they need to find it. I believe God intended it to be this way, because although you may not know it, we are all searching for God. The Bible tells us that man was made in the image of God, for direct communication with God, to speak to him face-to-face. And believe it or not, mankind misses God. We miss God because we all need Him – whether we are willing to admit it or not. C. S. Lewis called it the God-shaped gap - a hole inside each one of us - that can only be filled by God Himself.

People can feel the emptiness inside when trouble blows that gaping hole, meeting no resistance because God is not present. So what do they do? They search for a bubble to fill the hole. People spend their whole lives searching for God and not knowing it.

Chasing Him and passing Him by, many times, like the person who searches frantically for his glasses while all the time they are on his nose.

What about us Christians, who are satisfied that we are the church of the living God. We have accepted the truth of the gospel as our message and mission. Yet, there are people dying every day, not having found God, whom they have been searching for all their lives. We seem to have this 'If you can't beat them, join them' attitude. And so here we are, trying with all our might to force God out of the hole in our lives, that He would fill, if only we would let Him in, instead of trying to get bubbles to fill it. You may think you want to get married, but you are not looking for a spouse today, it is God you are searching for. You may think you want a big house and a flashy car, but it is God you really need. You may think you want all your debts to disappear and have more money than you know what to do with, but it is not financial security you are looking for, it is God you are searching for.

You may think you want letters after your name and a high-powered job, but it is God you really need. You may think you want to finish work early to live out the rest of your years in comfort in the sun, but it is not early retirement you look forward to - it is God, who is the basis of your hopes. Only God can make you achieve that fragile hope for a happy-ever-after life, even in the face of adversity. And when this life is over and God establishes His kingdom, only God can introduce you to a life that even your wildest dreams could never have conceived. Even the phrase, 'happy-ever-after' cannot adequately describe it. If the living God was worshipped and adored the world over, half as much as the royal corpse, we would all be up in heaven now having a big party.

The song says, "Jesus is the answer for the world today. Above Him there's no other – Jesus is the way." Yet, as Isaiah wrote, today Jesus is still despised and rejected of men (Isaiah 53:3), today people are still hiding, as it were, their faces from Him because they do not esteem Him. To those people I want to say, forget about the People's Princess, who is no more. Instead, I want to introduce you to Jesus, the Prince of Peace, who says to you today, "I have loved you with an everlasting love" (Jeremiah 31:3). He has already done more for you than any human ever could, and can continue to touch your lives in ways that you never dreamed were possible. All you have to do is say, "Lord, I'm here. I need you." He will fill your life with such sweetness that your bubble-chasing days will be over.

The scripture passage at the beginning of this chapter tells us that God is on trial today. Satan would have us believe that God does not really love us, but that all He cares about is having us keep every one of His rules or break them at our peril. Satan says that it is too hard to live a life of devotion to God. But we do not all believe that, because Jesus has shown us differently. So, Jesus is looking for witnesses, witnesses like Job who will not crack under pressure to forsake God, but rather declare, "…though he slay me yet will I trust Him" (Job 13:15). Witnesses who know God so well that He is an indistinguishable part of them, like Jeremiah, who declared, "His word was in my heart as a burning fire shut up in my bones. I was weary of holding it in and indeed I could not" (Jeremiah 20:9). Jesus is looking for witnesses who will testify of His love, like a man who was thought to be insane, who wrote this verse before he died:

Could we with ink the oceans fill
And were the skies of parchment made,

Were every stalk on earth a quill
And every man a scribe by trade.
To write the love of God above,
Would drain the oceans dry,
Nor could the scroll contain the whole
Though stretched from sky to sky.

Jesus is looking for witnesses. So if you want to be a witness for Jesus, bring your Bible and come. Get to know Him in His word and trust Him fully.

Stop chasing bubbles and start chasing God.
He'll always be there to the end.
Stop chasing bubbles and start chasing God
He is your Saviour and Friend.

Why would you scorn Him for Satan's trap?
Satan means you harm.
Only Jesus can fill your God-shaped gap
Be protected in His arms.

So, stop chasing bubbles and start chasing God
He'll fulfil your every need
When He frees you from all your cares
You'll truly be free indeed.

Stop chasing bubbles and chase God instead
And He will give you peace
For when you find God you'll find all your dreams
Your joy will never cease.

2

DREAM ON

Genesis 37:5; 39:2,3 ~ Proverbs 19:21

About a year ago I saw a film called "As Good As It Gets". The title comes from a scene where actor Jack Nicholson, playing an obsessive compulsive, bursts into his therapist's office, without an appointment, screaming for help. After he is turned away, his therapist refusing to consult with him, he interrupts a group session on his way out and remarks within the hearing of everyone, to no one in particular, "What if this is as good as it gets?"

That phrase haunted me. It was like a 'déjà vu' echo of the thoughts of billions of people around the globe. "What if this is as good as it gets?" is a question that many of us ask ourselves, when we are affected by tragedy - a question that is formed by the niggling uneasiness felt when one is forced to face the prospect of ones own mortality.

"What if this is as good as it gets?" was the question asked by many, when just after 7pm, on 21st December 1988, Pan American flight 103 blew apart in mid air and rained fire, debris, and bodies onto the town of Lockerbie, Scotland, killing 259 people on board and a further eleven residents on the ground. Grief-stricken relatives of the 270 people killed in the Lockerbie crash, waited eleven years for the case to come to trial, which only began in May 2000. What if this is as good as it gets?

Was the question people asked themselves in 1997, when the

world's favourite princess was killed, fleeing the menace of frenzied paparazzi, "What if this is as good as it gets?" Was this the question contemplated when two boys walked into Colombine High School in Littleton, Colorado, armed to the teeth and executed fifteen classmates before turning the guns on themselves?

Is this what his family and a black community were forced to wonder, when four white policemen shot Amadou Diallo, a harmless street peddler, 41 times? Nineteen bullets struck his body and snuffed out his life, and yet the four policemen were declared innocent of his murder.

"What if this is as good as it gets?" may have been the question on the minds of the people of Dunblane, Scotland, after Thomas Hamilton walked into the gym hall of Dunblane Primary School, with an assortment of high-powered hand guns and started spraying bullets. He killed kindergarten schoolteacher, Mrs Gwen Mayon, aged 45, and sixteen children, aged between 4 and 5 years. "What if this is as good as it gets?"

Was this the question on the minds of many when, in October 1999, around 30 people met their deaths as a result of driver error in the Paddington train crash? Fiona Macro, the daughter of a surviving passenger, wrote this poem entitled, *Signal 109*, and dedicated it to those who died or suffered as a result of the wreck.

Bent twisted metal deluges the remains
Of the soot-caked furnace that cremated the unlucky
The work-goers lie as dust beneath relatives' feet
Unable to answer their ever calling mobiles
That remain ringing in the survivors' ears

Images of death and pain, swamped the shocked minds
As the reality seeps deep into the weeping scars
That the survivors will never be able to heal
The seas of flowers wilt for the loved ones
That may never be found in the twisted urn.

"Is this as good as it gets?" asks the mums involved with the million-mum march for sensible gun laws in America. Mums like Linda Dattilo, whose six-year old twins were playing with neighbours in their backyard in Ocean City, New Jersey, when Linda heard "a horrific boom". In her own words she says, "I ran out and Allison was a fountain of blood. Half of her head was gone." A playmate had accidentally shot the girl with a .357 magnum that had been ditched by a fugitive under the Dattilo's porch the night before. And there was Mary Beth Hacke, whose family were devastated when a criminal opened fire on another car at the petrol station. One bullet struck Ryan Hacke, 14-months old, as his 3-year old brother looked on. Ryan died the next day. Is this as good as it gets?

"What if this is as good as it gets?" Is this the question on the mind of a couple who have sacrificed all their time, effort, energies, peace, happiness and purpose in life to a tragic event, which not only ended all prospects of a promising intelligent youth, but has now, 7 years on, also ended their marriage.

Neville and Doreen Lawrence were filled with despair over the brutal murder of their son, Stephen, on 22 April 1993. He was viciously attacked by white young men and left to die in the street. Despite long investigations, an aborted public prosecution and attempted private prosecution, no one has yet been convicted of his murder, or of any involvement in the attack on Stephen. Doreen Lawrence remarks, "Time has not been a healer for me."

Is this as good as it gets?

Today we talk about the dream, the power of the dream. What is it that lends to a dream enthusiasm, motivation and drive? Hope is the secret ingredient, the core, the beginning and sum total of a dream. Hope is what leads us to want to better ourselves, to better our society and to improve the world we live in. Hope is also what keeps us believing in an all powerful, omniscient, omnipresent God who holds the world in His hand.

A God who sits up high and looks down low. A God who knows the number of hairs on your head, who sees every act, hears every word, and records every thought, just as though there were only one person in the world, and the attention of all heaven were focused on him.

A God who so loved the human race that He sent His only Son to die in their place, so that they might be saved by amazing grace, if they should so desire. The dream that so many of us have today, the hope that burns within our hearts, is that, one day, Jesus will return to put an end to all suffering. So we are like strangers in a foreign land, not wanderers, but temporary residents, whose destination is the place that God has prepared for us.

There are, however, some people who have chosen to believe that this is as good as it gets. Like the translation of the film title in Spanish, they say *mejor imposible,* which means, *better impossible.* They have blinded themselves to the greatest dream, the only reality, the most sobering truth that we are always in the presence of God. They fail to realize that the things which are seen are temporal, but that the things which are not seen are eternal (2 Corinthians 4:18). They have rejected the power of the dream – hope, and in their hopelessness, they chose to believe that God is either no longer living, or does not exist, and that this life is all we have to look forward to. But despite these enemies of the dream, in spite of these hope-killers, God has a plan and He has given us all dreams. The realization of these dreams will speed up His plan and bring it to fruition.

Dreams appear a lot in the life story of Joseph, the son of Jacob, and they appear to affect the course of his life more markedly than any other character in the Bible. We read of him having two dreams as a boy (Genesis 37:5,9); interpreting two dreams in prison (Genesis 40:5); and then interpreting the two dreams of the pharaoh. Then, later, as the governor of Egypt, unrecognised by his brothers bowing before him, we read of him remembering the dreams he had as a boy (Genesis 41:1-6).

Each dream is a dream about the future; dreams like *you* have for the future. The Bible says that Joseph had a dream and when he told it to his brothers, they hated him all the more. Whenever you have a dream, or a vision or goal for something worthwhile, there will always be people who will hate you for it and they will try to stop you.

Dr Martin Luther King Jr. had a dream, and when he told it to his brothers they hated him all the more. Terry Waite had a dream and when he told it to his brothers they hated him too. Nelson Mandela had a dream and when he told it to his brothers, they hated him. Just like they hated Medger Evers, Malcolm X and Mamia Abu-Jamal. Even Princess Diana had a dream, a simple dream to get married again and start a new life, but some people were against her and against the man of her choice. So, that one kiss, caught on camera, was enough to excite the frenzy that caused her untimely end, leaving enough question marks to spell out the word “conspiracy” in the minds of many. Whenever you have a dream, there will always be people who will hate you for it and try to stop you. But dream on! The Bible says that Joseph had a dream, and when he told it to his brothers they hated him all the more.

Look at the suggestive wording of Genesis 37:5. It says, “they hated him all the more,” which means they already hated him with or without the dream. Why was that? If we do a little investigation into Joseph’s background, we find that his father, Jacob, had four wives. Polygamy had taken its toll on the family life: Rivalry between the wives had given birth to sibling rivalry among the sons. And because Joseph was the son of Jacob’s favourite wife, Rachel, and Jacob clearly loved him more than all his other children, a deep-seated, firmly rooted jealously sprang up in the hearts of his other sons. To make matters worse, Jacob gave Joseph the infamous technicolor dream-coat. A costly coat, such as was usually worn by persons of distinction, seemed to his other brothers to be further evidence of their father’s partiality. This excited a suspicion that Jacob intended to pass-by his elder children, to bestow the birthright of inheritance and clan leadership on the son of Rachel. A perfectly justified suspicion, if you remember that Jacob himself was the youngest child of his father. So, to add insult to injury, imagine this cheeky upstart of a boy telling his bigger brother, that he dreamt they were binding sheaves in the field when his sheaf stood upright while theirs bowed down and paid homage to his sheaf (Genesis 37:9–11).

The meaning of the dream is clear enough. “Let me get this straight – you are going to laud it over us? We’ll see about that!”, one brother threatened. The Bible says, “They hated him yet the more for his dreams and for his words.” Then Joseph dreamt another dream and fearlessly told his family that the sun, moon and eleven stars (the number of his brothers) bowed down and paid *him* homage. No subtlety with the sheaf going on here. And this time, even his father rebuked him, although he believed that God was revealing Joseph's future.

Joseph's brothers now hated him with a passion; they eyed him with contempt and called him 'the dreamer'. But they kept the extent of their hatred carefully hidden. One day, Joseph was sent to find his brothers, who were supposed to be tending the flocks in Shechem, the very place where Joseph's brothers had killed a whole city of men in revenge for the violation of their sister. Jacob sent Joseph in search of his brothers because he was worried for their safety. Jacob did not know their real feelings towards Joseph, otherwise he would have certainly thought twice about sending him!

Joseph journeyed for fifty miles (probably on foot) to Shechem, only to be directed to Dotham, another fifteen miles away. His brothers saw him approaching and they had no thought for the long journey their brother had made to see them. They were not happy to see him and the sight of his coat, evidence of their father's partiality, the token of his love, filled them with hatred.

"Here comes the dreamer," they mockingly said one to another. All the envy, all the bitterness, all the vengeful feelings towards the one prized above them in their father's affection, rose to the surface and began to control their outlook, removing all restraint as they drove pity from their hearts. Remember that these are ruthless men. They did not think twice about killing a whole city of men. Now they said, "Let's kill him," and they began to cherish the thought. "Yeah, let's kill him. We'll kill him and throw him in a pit and we'll say that some evil beast has devoured him; and what then shall become of his dreams?" That is what is so often the plan of those who are blind to the dream, *mejor imposible*. "Let's frustrate his plans in the worst way, make it impossible for his goal to be achieved. Let's kill him and we shall see what will become of his dreams."

William Wallace, "Let's kill him and we shall see what will become of his dreams." Abe Lincoln, "Let's kill him," they said. John Wycliffe, John Hus, "Let's kill him." Malcolm X, Medger Evers, "Let's kill him." John and Robert F Kennedy, "Let's kill him," they said. Mahatma Gandhi and Martin Luther King Jr., "Let's kill him, and we shall see what will become of his dreams."

The trouble is, it is easy enough to kill a man, nothing could be easier in the world, but how do you kill a dream?

T. E. Lawrence once said, "All men dream, but not equally. Those who dream by night in the dusty recesses of their minds awake to the day to find it was all vanity. But the dreamers of the day are *dangerous* men, for the many act out their dreams with open eyes, to make it possible."

How do you kill a dream? You can kill a man, but you cannot kill an idea. Make a martyr out of a man for his cause and ten will rise up to take his place. His dream ends up being more powerful than ever. So, his brothers said, "Let's kill him. We'll throw his body in a pit and we shall see what will become of his dreams." They would have done exactly that if *God* was not in control of the situation. God gave Joseph the dream, and him being killed in Dotham, was not part of His plan.

The Bible says that "God is not a man that He should lie, not the son of man that He should change His mind." (Numbers 23:19).

When God sets a plan in motion, it will come to be. God says, "So shall My word be that goes out of My mouth, it shall not return unto Me empty but shall accomplish that which I please" (Isaiah 55:11). When God said, "Let there be light," (Genesis 1:3) there was light and nothing could prevent that light from coming into being. When God speaks, action leaps into the fray. God's plan will always prevail.

So, Joseph arrived and was shocked and terrified by the murderous looks he found in the eyes of his brothers (Genesis 37:28). He was seized immediately and after that, things began to happen quickly. Before long, Joseph found himself a prisoner and a slave on his way to Egypt, in a caravan of Midianites, sold for a measly twenty pieces of silver. As far as realising his dream was concerned, all was marching splendidly according to plan. But poor Joseph did not know that. He did not even know what he wanted out of life.

All Joseph knew was that, to be a slave was, to him, a fate more to be feared than death. All along the journey, pictures of the hate-filled looks he received from his brothers flashed into his mind, and the insulting words that met his begging and pleading continued to ring in his ears. As he faced the prospect of separation from his father and his home, his grief and fear must have been immense. But God was in control, as He always is. When we experience failure, when tragedy rocks our worlds, we must remember that God is in control. There is nothing to be afraid of. This is just another piece of education on the journey that he has set me on. All is going according to plan. In effect, this is what Joseph did. Our story indicates that he did the least human thing to do. Instead of lamenting the injustice, he dedicated himself to God and accepted his lot, humbly.

Joseph was magnanimous! I don't know about you but if I was in Joseph's situation, I would be shouting, "Hello, God? Are You up there? Are You seeing this? Do You still care what happens to me? Then why? Why me?" Do you ever have your 'why' times? Like, "You disappoint me God. Why me? Why am I the one to get laid off?" or "Why is it so hard for me to find a job? Why me? Why do I have cancer? You disappoint me, God! I thought You cared! I thought You were a good God. Why did my husband leave me? Are you up there? Are You hearing this? Why did my mother die? Why didn't You take one of the murderers or rapists?" Am I the only one to have 'why me' times? God can handle your 'why me?' times. If you are waiting for an answer, His answer is always the same: Psalm 46:10 says, "Be still and know that I am God."

Joseph did not say, "Look God, when you are not busy, I would appreciate you doing something about this." Joseph applied himself to his work in Potiphar's house. In fact, he threw himself completely into his work and God so blessed his efforts that even his master had to sit up and take notice. Potiphar realised and accepted that God's favour was the secret of his unprecedented and unparalleled prosperity. The Bible says, "The Lord was with Joseph and he was a prosperous man… and his master saw that the Lord was with him and that He made all that he did to prosper in his hand" (Genesis 39:3,4).

Joseph's life is a witness to the fact that if you side with God, God will side with you. He lifts you onto His shoulders, He gives you wings to fly and He will give you great rewards just for trusting in Him. Isaiah 40:31 says, "…those who hope in the Lord will renew their strength, they will soar on wings like eagles, they will run and not grow weary, they will walk and not be faint."

That is the power of the dream.

Ah, but hold on a minute. If we read on a little further we see that Joseph is in jail. Now what in the world is Joseph, Mr Perfect, doing residing at His Majesty's pleasure? It is true that it was not his fault. Potiphar's wife tried to get him to sleep with her and when he would not, she lied and said that he had assaulted her. So, Joseph is in jail. Of course, if Potiphar had even the slightest suspicion that his wife was telling the truth Joseph would have been executed immediately, but he knew Joseph and it was not consistent with his character. Still Potiphar's dignity had to be preserved - Joseph was thrown into prison for a crime he did not commit. This is all the more reason why you would think God would come to his rescue. After all, we all know he sent an angel to free Peter. If you were Joseph, wouldn't you think it absolutely ludicrous to assume that it is God's will that you stay in prison? But no rescue came for Joseph, he was left to rot in prison.

What a fall from grace! From respected head of an important household, to being treated as a common criminal, and just when he was beginning to think things were going well for him. But God was not yet finished with Joseph. God had bigger plans for him. God had to prepare him in the school of affliction, where he would witness the results of oppression, tyranny and crime and learn lessons of justice, sympathy and mercy that would prepare him to exercise power with wisdom and compassion. And this is where Joseph's story really becomes our story.

We all have to go through troubles. God tests us to make us stronger and to equip us for the big plans He has for us. We all have obstacles in our paths on our journey through life, towards our dream. We all have to study in the school of hard knocks, but God is always in control and all is according to plan.

All of us react to the fire of adversity in different ways. You can choose how you are going to react to a crisis, in the same way that different materials react to real fire. You can be burned like paper – just burnt up inside and be of no use to anybody or anything. Or you can harden like clay and become a menace to society – incapable of giving, feeling, letting anything through your impervious boundaries. You can melt like wax, completely the opposite, becoming a softie with no backbone, unwilling to take risks. Or you can become refined, like gold – more valuable and much better for the experience.

The best way to be like the gold, is to recognise and accept, like Joseph, that God is in control, that trouble happens for a reason. God has a plan and He has not forgotten about you, nor the dreams He gave you.

Jeremiah recognised this when he said, "O Lord, I know that the way of man is not himself; it is not in man who walks to direct his steps" (Jeremiah 10:23). There may be many setbacks along the way, but they are fuel for the dream and strength for the resolve. As one speaker said, "If it ain't trouble, it ain't no good." It takes time and patience to build a dream. This reminds me of a fragment of a poem.

"With a lusty yell and a ho-heave-ho
They swung a beam and a whole wall fell.
I said to the foreman, "Are these men skilled
And of the type you'd use if you had to build."
He just laughed and said, "No.
Indeed common labour is all I need.

I could easily tear down in a day or two
What skilled men took a year to do."

But building a dream, achieving a goal, realising an ambition, takes assiduousness and tenacity, blood, sweat and tears, dedication and perspiration, and that is why so many people spend their time tearing down dreams and hindering the progress of others, because it is so much easier to do.

It is easier to discourage than to encourage; easier to destroy confidence than to build it; easier to put down than to lift up.

But I say to you, dream on. Do not let the dreamless and the hopeless discourage you. You cannot just let them win with an "If you can't beat 'em, join 'em" attitude, and say that this is as good as it gets. You cannot just give up and say, "Mejor… imposible" – I can't do better than this.

What if Thomas Edison had said, "Mejor...imposible, man"? We would not be able to take for granted the recording and reproduction of the human voice and instant light at the flick of switch. What if the Wright brothers and others had said, "Mejor…imposible"? What if these two bicycle engineers had agreed with those who were saying, "If man were meant to fly, God would have given him wings." We would not be able to reach other continents in a matter of hours, or the other side of the world in a little over a day.

There are a few evangelists who have their own private jets. How is that for a gospel tool? What if Dr Daniel Hale Williams, the pioneer Black surgeon, who performed the world's first open heart surgery in 1893 had said, "Mejor…imposible!" What if Dr Charles Drew who developed the blood bank system had said,

"Mejor…imposible!" What if NASA, after the Soviet Union were the first to put a man in space, had said, "Mejor… imposible!" We would not know the first words of the first moonwalker – long before Michael Jackson – "One small step for man, one giant leap for mankind." What if Donna Dees-Thomases, mother to two young children, who have been victims of gun violence, had said, "Mejor…imposible!" There would not have been 750,000 mums marching on Mothers' Day, 14th May in Washington DC, campaigning for the use of common sense by a nation in love with the gun – a campaign which was taken very seriously by opponents and supporters alike.

Dreams come from God and we should never listen to those who would have us give them up. Winston Churchill, Charles Darwin, G. K. Chesterton, Thomas Edison and Albert Einstein would not be the famous people they are today if they had listened to friends, family and educators who told them, "Mejor…imposible!"

As a youth, Winston Churchill seemed so dull that his father thought he might be incapable of earning a living in England. Charles Darwin did so poorly in school that his father once told him, "You will be a disgrace to yourself and all your family."
G. K. Chesterton, the English writer, could not read until he was 8. One of his teachers told him, " If we could open your head we should not find any brain, but only a lump of white fat." Thomas Edison's first teacher described him as "addled" and his father almost convinced him to believe that he was a "dunce." Albert Einstein's parents feared that their child was dull and he performed so badly in all high school courses, except mathematics, that a teacher asked him to drop out. These men 'made it' because of their determination. They took hard knocks and they got beaten down, but they got up and kept going.

The value of courage, persistence and perseverance has rarely been illustrated more convincingly than in the life story of this man:

Failed in business at 22
Ran for legislature – defeated at 23
Again failed in business – at 24
Elected to legislature at 25
Sweetheart died at 26
Had a nervous breakdown at 27
Defeated for speaker at 29
Defeated for elector at 31
Defeated for Congress at 34
Elected for Congress at 37
Defeated for Congress at 39
Defeated for Senate at 46
Defeated for Vice President at 47
Defeated for Senate at 49
Elected President of the United States at 51

That is the record of Abraham Lincoln. Imagine that!

But look what comes from the diary of John Wesley, brother of Charles Wesley, famous for hymns.

Sunday am, May 5
Preached in St Anne's was asked not to come back anymore.

Sunday pm, May 5
Preached in St John's. Deacons said, "Get out and stay out!"

Sunday am, May 19
Preached in St Somebody Else's. Deacons called a special

meeting and said I couldn't return.

Sunday pm, May 19
Preached on street. Kicked off street.

Sunday am, June 2
Preached out at edge of town. Kicked off highway.

Sunday pm, June 2
Afternoon preached in a pasture. 10,000 people came out to hear me.

When you have a dream that is sacred, it comes from God, and you have got to put your all into achieving it. Never say, "mejor…imposible!" Never say, "I can't." They say triumph is just 'umph' added to 'try.'
When trouble comes, you have to face it, take it in your stride, grit your teeth, get your head down, press forward and dream on. And remember, God is in control.

God promises,

> "When you pass through the waters, I will be with you and through the rivers, they shall not overflow you; when you walk through the fire you will not be burned, nor the flame scorch you" (Isaiah 43:2).

There have been times over the past year or so when I have thought "es que no puedo más." Literally translated it means, "It's because I can't move." This time it wasn't, "Why me?", it was more like, "Woe is me." The death of my brother a couple of years back wreaked havoc on my degree programme, because I had to put all my exams off until the next available opportunity. I went out to Spain with courses hanging over my head. I came back failing to finish the designated extended essay and experiential learning analysis, then went straight into my final year, piling up more work for myself. I fell ill, failing miserably at the Herculean task of getting my assignments in, and I missed my exams. And I thought, "*I just can't take it anymore*." I haven't been back to any classes since December. And so, at the behest of my parents and all my friends, I was told go and see my lecturers and tell them of my plight. Being a big institution, (I attended classes on two separate campuses, some miles apart) the faculty knew nothing about me. I was overawed and overwhelmed at the prospect of the 'red tape' I would have to face. I wrote a tentative e-mail to one of the assessment administrators and I received no reply. My friend begged me, "…go in before it's too late because if the term ends before you sort it out and you're wanting to go back in October, it's all over."

So, I phoned and a person advised me to go to the Campus Student Advice Centre to speak to a Duty Advisor. I booked an appointment, and saw her on Thursday [11 May 2000]. I was expecting to be given the 'third degree' about why I had not contacted them in six months, but I was not. She did not even ask for medical certificates. I felt that God was with me. She wrote a letter to the relevant people on the spot and she devised a way for me to come back the following year to do the modules that were outstanding, and the deferrals. She also applied for all the nine grades that had 'incomplete without good reason' to be changed. And for the first time I really started to realise that it was not impossible. Even though I thought it was all over, God was in control. For the first time it really looked as if God was directing me, showing me a way out.

Jesus was the Man with the plan and He was really going to help me out of the hole I'd dug for myself. I thought, *"no puedo más. I've taken all I can take. I can't take anymore."* But I was wrong. Isaiah tells us, "He gives power to the faint, and to them that have no might, He gives increased strength" (Isaiah 40:29).

There were times when any other normal person in Joseph's position would have thought, "God has forgotten about me." Even after God gave him the interpretation of the dream of the king's own butler, he was left rotting in the dungeon. He thought he was in the clear because he asked the butler to mention his name to the pharaoh. In time he gave up hope. The butler had obviously forgotten. But God was not ready for him to leave prison, just yet.

It was a full two years before Joseph received a summons to the palace. His destiny had finally arrived (Genesis 41:14). God had chosen him to be governor of Egypt, subject only to pharaoh at a time when Egypt was the most powerful nation of the ancient world. And when he saw his brothers bowing before him, the Bible says that he remembered the dreams God gave him as a boy (Genesis 42:9), and no doubt realised the purpose for what he had had to go through.

Joseph's life is proof of the truth of the statement in Proverbs 16:9: "A man's heart plans his way, but the Lord directs his steps." 'But' is an interesting conjunction here. It tells us that the second clause that comes is about to change the meaning of the first clause. For example, Proverbs 14:12, "There is a way that seems right to a man, *but* its end is the way of death." Note how the first clause is seen in a different context and how the second takes on a different significance. This is also demonstrated in Proverbs 16:9, "A man's heart plans his way *but* the Lord directs his steps". And Proverbs 19:21, "Many are the plans in a man's heart *but* it is the Lord's purpose that prevails."

My message to you, therefore, is to dream on, but dedicate your dreams to God. Trust Him and surrender to His plan. He gives strength to the weary and increases the power of the weak. Even young people grow tired and weary and young men stumble and fall; *but* those who hope in the Lord will renew their strength. They will soar on wings like eagles; they will run and not grow weary, they will walk and not be faint (Isaiah 40:29-31).

God has singled you out to do great things and to stand before kings.

Why would you refuse God's plan,
A plan to guide you across your span of life
That foes may not withstand
The progress of the Man with the plan.

Guided by the Saviour's life
To run roughshod over trouble and strife
And be different from the world and it's wife,
To be found in the Way, the Truth and the Life.

Never from His path will He let you stray
To be Christian in all you do and say
To seek Him each and every day
And be proof that Jesus is the Way.

If you decide each and every day to trust in God, whatever happens, you can always be content that all is going according to plan.

3

CAN'T COOK! WON'T COOK! DEATH IN THE POT!

Three young boys lived in the mountains of North Carolina. One July day, they decided to go berry picking. With them was their baby brother, who was about nine months old. Putting the baby on the cool, short grass near the berry bushes, the boys went to work. The baby was within sight of them and from time to time they would peer through the bushes to see whether all was well.

Busy chatting and eating berries, while putting a few in their buckets, the boys heard the baby chattering to himself in baby talk, as babies do. But, on hearing him laugh, they peered through the bushes. It appeared he was petting something: a huge rattlesnake lay across their little brother's legs. His tiny hands were stroking the snake's smooth skin; its scaly face was very close to the baby's but the child felt no fear at a sight that would have struck terror in the heart of a full-grown man. The boys looked on in horror! What should they do? They decided to do nothing, realising that to disturb the snake could mean a convulsing and excruciating demise for the baby in less than 10 minutes. The baby kept talking in soft tones, patting the sleek body. Finally, after what seemed a very long time to the watching boys, the snake slithered away into the tall grass.

As sinful humans, sometimes we mess around with things we have no business messing with. Like babies, who have no concept of danger, we too get mixed up in situations where we meddle with things we have no understanding of, and act without knowing what or whom we are dealing with. Sometimes a thing can look good on the outside. You know, the things that the world has to offer, look great and they seem innocent enough. But when you get into it, nothing but self-destruction is their reward, and death and judgment await you on the other side!

A Shakespearean tale tells of a beautiful heiress whose father devised a test for all her suitors. If they succeeded, they would win her hand in marriage, but if they failed, they had to leave and vow celibacy for the rest of their lives.

The test:
A room contained 3 caskets, one of gold, one of silver and one of lead. Only one casket could be chosen and if it were found to contain her portrait, then the test was over and happiness assured. One such suitor chose the golden casket because of its appearance and the inscription bore the words, "Who chooses me will gain what many men desire." But when he opened it all he found was a skeleton with a piece of paper in the socket of one eye, on which was written:

All that glisters is not gold
Often you have heard that told
Many a man his life hath sold
Just my outside to behold
Gilded tombs do worms infold
Had you been as wise as bold
Young in limbs, in judgement old
Your answer had not been inscrolled
Fare you well, your suit is cold.

Never could a greater parallel be found for the Christian life. The wise writer of Proverbs tells us that, "There is a way which seems right to a man, but the ends thereof are the ways of death" (Proverbs 14:12).

Let us focus for a while on the subject "Can't Cook, Won't Cook!"

It begins: 'There was a famine in the land....' A story of this kind always starts this way, because that is how deadly mistakes begin. It begins with a famine, a picture of destitution, a shortage of sustenance, a paucity of provisions, which are essential to the appeasement of the soul's hunger and to the supplying of what life lacks.

There is a famine in the land, a modern day famine in a modern time land, where there is a lack of wholesome food for thought, a shortage of spiritual sustenance. There is a famine in the land. A land where people's only comfort were material morsels and luxurious leftovers. There is a famine in the land – destitution that men and women bring on themselves, waxing eloquently about evolution and giving their allegiance to atheism.

There is so great a famine in the land that its far-reaching effects have even impacted the school of the prophets and it has made itself known here in the church. And, men and women go out in search of food. Look at the story in 2 Kings 4:38-41. In verse 38, we see Elisha arriving in Gilgal. The sons of the prophets are there and he tells his servant to put on a big pot of stew for them. In verse 39, one man goes out into the field to gather herbs for the stew. Now remember, there is a famine, so there's not likely to be an abundance of anything terrific to eat, but his search is rewarded by the discovery of a wild vine not of grapes but of gourds. The exact kind is not certain, but commentators say that the gourd in question seems to identify with the fruit of the colocynth, a gourd-like plant which creeps along the ground, and has a round yellow fruit about the size of a large orange. This fruit is exceedingly bitter, produces colic, and affects the nerves. This culinary cretin gathers as many as he can fit into the large fold of his cloak and goes off as happy as the legendary Larry. Back at the pot, he chops up his toxic tucker.

Can't cook! Won't cook! is a cooking competition involving those who do not know how to and those who could not care less about it; neither have any culinary expertise. Can't cook! Won't cook!

This message goes out to two types of person: the ignorant and those who couldn't care less.

God is concerned about us who go out into the field to gather herbs to 'spice up our life', as it were, forgetting that this world is not our home and that we are just a-passing through. So, a young person goes out into the field, goes off to university, far away from home and their parents. You make new friends, non-Christian friends, too. There is nothing wrong with that. But as is so often the case, rather than you having a lasting impact on your non-Christian friends, changing some of their practices, you find yourself doing things that you never would have done before. You find that what you had when you lived at home, were not standards but customs and traditions, which are hard to keep up, away from their contextual source.

You can never make non-Christians understand why you do not do certain things. So, you will start to question, rethink and convince yourself that compromise is the way to go. They will tell you that nicotine is more addictive than ganja; they will not tell you that smoking one spliff is like smoking ten cigarettes in terms of its powerful effects on the nervous system. They will tell you that scientifically, it is proven that alcohol in small quantities, as with the case of a glass of red wine a day, with a meal, actually lessens the likelihood of developing heart disease. They will tell you that a glass of white wine a day will help your lung capacity. They will not tell you that alcohol in any quantity kills brain cells that will never be regenerated. They will tell you that psychoactive, psychedelic drugs expand the mind and alter the perception, that it will add a new horizon to your outlook on life; they will tell you that Nobel prizes have been won and revolutionary advances in the world of information processing have been made while academics were on drugs. But what they will not tell you is that every day drugs ruin many young lives.

Death to your prospects means death to your peace of mind. Death in the pot! 2 Kings 4: 40 says, "The stew was poured out for the men, but as the began to eat it, they cried out, 'O man of God, there is death in the pot!' And they could not eat it." They didn't know what the problem was. All they could see was food before them, and they were hungry! But the Bible says it so happened that as they were eating, a scene from of a wedding caterer's nightmare began to unfold. Distorted expressions of distaste began to appear on the faces of the diners, as winces and groans escaped from their lips as the horror of nausea and revulsion lead to that of discomfort and pain. Folk began to collapse and to writhe on the ground, clutching their stomachs with terror and in agony, as the deadly stew took effect.

As if by shared single thought, folks began to scatter in search of the longer grass, sticking fingers down their throats, noisily seeking to unburden themselves of the acrid edibles. And as the guttural sounds of choking filled the air, loud gasps were heard as folks cried out, with a note of incredulity in their voices, "O man of God, there is death in the pot!"

Can't cook! Won't cook! Whether we are unaware of what we are doing or getting ourselves into, or really couldn't care less, it is we who eat the stew; it is we who bring trouble upon ourselves, looking to the world, and behaviour associated with the world to spice up our lives. Can't cook. Won't cook. We are both ignorant, willingly or unwillingly so. We are both gullible, and taken by the oh-so-familiar phrase "There's nothing wrong with it." We are in grave danger. Our minds are like an open pot: willing recipients of scenes of violence and sex on the screen, accompanied by the sounds of explicit expletives.

Death is mixed in the pot with years of loud music slowly destroying the hearing, and damaging our spiritual hearing, to devastating effect, with lyrics of innuendo and satanic verses. Still we party on, surrounded by those dedicated to his hedonistic philosophy. "Hey it looks good, it feels good, there's nothing wrong with it." Death in the pot!

Can't cook. Won't cook! They are materialistic too! Some want to work hard for it and then build bigger barns and sit back and enjoy the fruit of their labours, while their heavenly coffers go empty. And some are dedicated to the quick fix solution, whether it be gambling or cheating or stealing or fraud. They scorn the blessings of God and keep back tithes and offerings. They are unwilling helpers and bad stewards, dedicated solely to their own earthly comfort in thought, ambition, and outlook. Death in the pot!

Can't cook! Won't cook! They are vulnerable in the area of human relations, so they step on a path that has a beginning and an end. It all starts with the occasional touching, then the hugging and the kissing. And once a couple begin to do the hide and seek game, then they have taken a course wittingly or not, that ends in pre-marital sex and it can only end in tears.

There's nothing wrong with it. Ignorance!
There's nothing wrong with it. Foolishness!
There's nothing wrong with it. Danger!
There's nothing wrong with it. A recipe for disaster. Death in the pot!

But the story is not all bad news. You see, when those sons of the prophets, thanks to the taste buds that God had given them, discovered the bitter aftertaste, they knew something was amiss. When you or I are in trouble, when we are experiencing the aftertaste of bitter experience, the next step that is so vital to the soul's survival, is to realise and admit that we are in trouble and that we need help. Then Jesus will come to the rescue. Jesus, who is both the Master Physician and the Miracle Medicine; Jesus, who is both the Master Chef and Secret Ingredient, will turn that situation around so that what we thought would kill us, will in effect cure us. Jesus will turn it around, so what we thought would beat us, will treat us. It will not break us, it will make us.

But we have got to want His help. Believe it or not, many of us do not want to be cured. We search for anything and everything. We reject Him over and over and are convinced we do not need Him. But the bitter aftertaste reveals death in the pot! There is death in the pot, yet we continue to eat. Death in the pot, yet we believe it tastes sweet.

Death in the pot: we go on despite the hurt. Death in the pot: still we leave the church. There is death in the pot, you may warn them in vain. Death in the pot, yet they will not refrain.

But the story ends on a positive note. After they cried out and said, "O man of God there is death in the pot", 2 Kings 4: 41 tells us that Elisha commanded that some cornmeal be brought and put into the pot of stew. After that, they poured out some of the stew and everyone did eat, with no adverse effects.

A difference can be made in our lives when Jesus is added to the mixture. Like the cornmeal, Jesus soaks up the poison. Jesus declared himself the essential foodstuff of survival, when he said, "Except you eat the flesh of the son of man and drink his blood, you have no life in you." He also said, "He that eats my flesh and drinks my blood dwells in me and I in him."

If Jesus does not live inside us, if we do not invite Him to come into our lives, then we will reap the bitter harvest of the seeds sown - seeds of self-destruction and disobedience. You have got to seek Jesus, beg Him to influence your life. Look for Him. Talk to Him, day-by-day, hour-by-hour, minute-by-minute, second-by-second, moment-by-moment, micron-by-micron. A moment is 56/1000ths of a second, and the song says, "Moment by moment we're kept in His love." What an encouraging and comforting thought!

It is only by keeping Jesus in your life that you can ensure that nothing you bring upon yourself will ruin you. You will continue to experience trouble, but those experiences will not ruin, they will only refine, because there is cleansing power in the pot.

4

REPENTANCE

Luke 15:11-20

Here we have the well-known story that Jesus told. The father in the story, has two sons. The youngest of which, probably in his late teens or early twenties, was a little restless.

All of us, at some time in our lives experience this same restlessness. We may feel that we're not doing enough with our lives; that there is not enough action in our lives; that we are not moving far enough towards meeting our ambitions; that there is a lack of excitement in our lives and as a result, we are left feeling restless.

One of the main contributors to this restlessness is that we seem to go through phases in our lives where we search for our identity. A search, which hopefully answers questions like: Who am I? What am I doing here? And where am I going?

A young person can usually find answers to these questions that satisfy them at their stage of development. But during a lifetime, at various stages of life, we find ourselves experiencing this type of restlessness over and over again. We find ourselves searching for answers to the great questions of life.

It seems that our lives go round in cycles. Once we have found our identity and answered the great questions at one stage of life, there then comes another period of time when we no longer feel content and satisfied and we start to wonder and search all over again for the reasons why we feel restless and restricted. We come to a place where we feel that something is hindering our enjoyment and freedom. And so our quest is to identify the source of our restraint, which comes in the form of a tension, leading to a build up of anger, resentment, jealousy and bitterness - a huge bomb of emotions. Then one final conflict ignites the fuse and the unsuspecting victim, in this case the father, is left to feel the force of all our bottled up feelings, which ends up severing the link between us.

It seems as though you are being given a lecture in developmental psychology. But really, I am suggesting to you that the plight of the prodigal son, may have led him to say, *Father, give me the portion of goods that belongs to me*. Somehow, he identifies his father as the source of discomfort and restlessness. Out of the blue, he demands of his father, "Give me what is mine. Give me what you have for me. I've had it with this life. I'm sick and tired of slaving for you as a workhorse. I don't want to waste my life working for you. I want to enjoy my life before I'm too old. Give me what's mine. I don't want to wait around until you die! Give me the money now!"

And what did the Father say? (I know what I would have said: "Look 'ere boy! Is who you tink you talking to? You better get out fast before me lick you down? You forgot you place? Is something wrong with you?")

The Bible says in Luke 15:12,
"And the younger of them said to his father, Father, give me the portion of goods that belongs to me. And he divided between them his living."
In other words the father gave him exactly what he requested. I might have given him what he deserved, but the father bowed to

his demand. We might well ask what kind of father gives in like that? What kind of father lets his son get away with that?

And yet, our heavenly father does exactly the same for us. Matthew 11: 29 says, "He is meek and lowly in heart." He doesn't force us to do anything. He doesn't tell anybody that they are too young to run their own life. He just says, "Okay. If that's your decision, I won't stand in your way."
He says, "If you are going to serve me, I want you to serve me wholeheartedly, not half-heartedly. I don't want you to feel forced or even obliged to serve me. I want you to serve me out of love."

Ellen White says, in Steps to Christ, p.44,

> "There are those who profess to serve God, while they rely upon their own efforts to obey His law, to form a right character, and secure salvation. Their hearts are not moved by any deep sense of love of Christ, but they seek to perform the duties of the Christian life as that which God requires of them to gain heaven. Such religion is worth nothing. The [person] who attempts to keep the commandments of God from a sense of obligation merely because he is required to do so will never enter into the joy of obedience."

God never forces us to do anything. You know the rest of the story - how the son left and went into a far country. You know how he entered into a riotous lifestyle. He pursued a course of life, which said: 'Live it up. Party till you drop. Have a good time now. Live it up.' It is a philosophy that is gaining more and more popularity in this world. 'Have fun. Pleasure is the be-all and end-all of life.' You know how he ended up on that roller coaster of life, which is based on, 'if it feels good, do it - whatever makes you happy!' And this roller coaster lifestyle is such that when you are up oh it's good, when you are on top the feeling is great. But, when you eventually hit the bottom of the roller coaster lifestyle, your very existence is turned upside down and inside out; your life feels like its not worth living.

This son, this prodigal son, rode on this roller coaster of life, for the Bible says, "And not many days after the younger son gathered all together; and took his journey into a far country, and there wasted his substance with riotous living" (Luke 15:13).

You can see him as he walks away from home. Pressed. Dressed to kill in his Pierre Cardin suit, smelling of Dolce and Gabbana cologne, walking in his Russell and Bromley brogues, with his Rolex watch on his wrist and his Samsonite attaché case in his other hand.

You can see him as he walks away from the safety and security of home. You can see him as he walks down that road, which is so far from what his home, his father and family stand for. You can see him as he embarks on that road that can only lead to destruction, a life of 'riotous living' - the road that leads to a life of sin.

Luke 15:14a says, "And when he had spent all..." If we are honest, we have all come to that place. The place where we find ourselves helpless and hopeless, although God wishes us no ill, staring at the consequences of our bad decisions.

"And when he had spent all, there arose a mighty famine in that land; and he began to be in want."

Sin causes us to be just that. It causes us to be in want. How many of us after experiencing the wake-up call that the

consequences of sin brings, begin 'to be in want', wishi
could turn back the clock, wishing that we could go bac
things differently. Wishing that we had stayed at home in the place of security and safety.

The Bible describes how drastic his plight was, by saying in Luke 15:15, 16 “And he went and hired himself to a citizen of that country, who sent him to his fields to feed pigs. And he yearned to fill his belly with the husks that the pigs were eating: and no man gave him anything.”

What a situation to be in.

The story goes, a farmer once went to buy a mule from a neighbouring farmer.
"Is it a good mule," he asked.
"Oh, yes, it is a very good mule. In fact it will work all day without any trouble."
"You mean, I won't have to beat it to make it go and it will work all day long."
"That's right. No beating. It will just work on its own."
So the farmer bought the animal, and took it home. Early the next morning, he hitched it to the plough, eager to try out his new acquisition. But the mule would not budge. Not one inch. The farmer pulled, he pushed, he coaxed and finally he cursed the animal in his frustration, but still that stubborn mule would not move.

Just then the man, from whom the farmer had bought the mule, came down the road beside the field.
"Say!" yelled the farmer indignantly. I thought you said this animal would work all day without any trouble, but this beast won't move."

"He'll go," called back the former owner. "Here I'll start him for you!" and he rode over to the reluctant mule, picking up a small stick on the way. When he reached the animal, he whacked it over the head with the stick. With a lunge, the mule started forward and worked all day with no fuss.

"Well!" said the farmer, when he saw the man again. "That mule certainly works well, once it gets started. But I thought you said, I wouldn't have to hit it to make it work."
"You don't," was the answer. "But you must get its attention first."

Right there in that smelly, slushy pigsty, God caught that young man's attention. How many boys and girls are like that mule - they have good brains but don't study. Their teachers push and pull and coax, all to no avail. They have to be whacked over the head with a failing grade or a lecture from their parents to wake them up.

And you can be sure that God sometimes permits us to be whacked over the head, so to speak, with an accident or a death in the family, for example, so that He can get our attention.

The Bible says, in Luke 15:17, "And when he had come to himself..."
God knows how to get our attention. He knows how to get us to wake-up. And right there in that pigsty God got his attention.

Picture it: He is there in that pigsty, his prospects are looking bleak, and he's made a mess of his life. Sin leads you to make such a mess. Think about it as a pigsty. There is nothing pleasant about pigs. All we can say about pigs is that they smell. And if you are around pigs long enough you too will smell. Similarly, if you are around sin long enough you too will indulge.

But God is there, calling him to his senses. His suit has gone threadbare; his shoes are worn out; he has no use for his attaché case; his cologne has faded out, but God is still calling him to himself. His life is in a mess, but God still brings him to himself. You see, just as the Pierre Cardin suit, and the Russell and Bromley brogues, and the Rolex watch had no place in the pigsty, neither had he. He was born for better things.

God called him to himself and there and then he recognised what a terrible mistake he had made. He knew what he had to do and where he had to go, if he were to have any hope. "And he arose, and came to his father" (Luke 15:20).

He had walked swiftly away from his father in glee, as he had his inheritance. But now the road back was a long one. He had time to think and contemplate. He had to walk back now, along the very road of riotous living. He remembered the places where he had overindulged, wasted his time and substance; the places where he experienced the popularity that wealth brings. He remembers all the places where he let himself down.

In my mind's eye, I picture him talking to himself as he walks back home. I picture him putting himself down as he considers what his father will say.
"I told you so."
"I did not send you anywhere."
"You made your bed so lie in it."
"What do you want from me now!"

That walk back must have been very long, as he tried to predict how he would be treated.

Years ago, a bridge was to be built across New York Harbour. The engineers were having considerable difficulty in finding a solid foundation for one of the buttresses. Right where they wanted to put the support, they found an old boat, whose flat, rectangular hull was filled with brick and stones. The old barge was nearly buried in mud. Divers went down and put great heavy chains under the brittle boat. They tried every modern method to raise the sunken boat, but all their efforts failed.

Nearing the point of desperation, the experienced engineers were approached by a young engineer who was just beginning his career.

"I think I have a plan that will succeed. May I try?"

They listened to his plan and were convinced, and told him to proceed. Two large barges went back to the spot. Again, chains were placed under the old sunken barge, attached to the two barges and winched up tightly during the low tide. Now came the test.

Anxiously, the engineers stopped everything as they waited for the tide to come in. They noticed that the barges began to rise slowly. The old boat, so heavily loaded with bricks and stones and stuck in the mud, could not resist this mighty power of nature. Gradually, it was raised by the tide that lifted the two barges.

What human genius could not do, God's mighty power, manifested in nature, did, just as simply as a child might pick up a fallen toy. This power, which is in the ocean, I believe can be in your life too. We try to resolve our wrong doings in our own way, and end up making a mess. We simply need to rely on God's power and turn everything over to Him. Our part is to stop and wait for God to act.

I believe that was the best thing that son ever did – head back home to his father. But, I also believe that that was the hardest and longest road he travelled. The road of repentance always is, but it has sure rewards. For the Bible says, in Luke 15:20, "And he arose and came to his father. But when he was a great way off, his father saw him, and had compassion, and ran, and fell on his neck, and kissed him."

You can say the prodigal took a step in the right direction. Though he sauntered home, wondering what the outcome would be. Though he ambled home wishing for, at least, food and shelter, the Bible says his father saw him from a great way off. Though he walked to his father, his father ran to meet him. Though he smelt like a pig, his father put his arms around him. Though he had no right to enter back on his father's land, his father gave him a welcome that said, "I missed you."

When we take that step that leads to repentance, our Father *runs* to meet us, puts His *arms around us* and says, "Son, I missed you." "Daughter, I missed you."

What an expression of love. What a demonstration of acceptance. An action that states, in no uncertain terms: "There is, therefore, no condemnation to them which are in Christ Jesus, who walk not after the flesh, but after the Spirit."

The songwriter, so aptly penned the words, which epitomise the prodigal's experience:

I was sinking deep in sin,
Far from the peaceful shore,
Very deeply stained within,
Sinking to rise no more,
But the Master of the sea,
Heard my despairing cry,
From the waters lifted me,
Now safe am I.

Love lifted me!
Love lifted me!
When nothing else could help
Love lifted me!

Repentance is all about love. It's about turning to a Father who invites us and welcomes us to His table. We come to Him with our sins confessed. He forgives us, and we can leave His table as though we had never sinned.

'When nothing else could help, Love lifted me.'

5

SANCTIFIED WEAKNESS

2 Corinthians 12: 9,10

Sailors, in the 1800's, dreaded the dangerous French Pass, off the coast of New Zealand. Here, the six-mile-long channel between the two islands that make up New Zealand, was full of treacherous currents and jagged rocks that were concealed, just below the surface. Many ships were lost in this region.

One stormy morning, in 1871, the Brindle, sailing from Boston to Sydney, was having trouble going through the Pass, when a porpoise leapt out of the water. The men wanted to harpoon it, but the captain's wife suggested they follow it. Being experienced sailors, these men didn't want to listen to a woman, let alone follow a mammal of the dolphin family. Still, they knew that the porpoise had spent its life in these treacherous waters. For years it had plied swiftly through the open channels, avoiding the rocks. Yes, it knew a lot more about the channel (the Sound) than the sailors did. So, putting aside selfish pride and human judgement, they humbly followed the porpoise and made a safe passage.

From that time, Pelorus Jack, as they called the porpoise, stayed around the Sound. Sailors watched for him. As soon as the porpoise saw a ship it leapt out of the water and was always greeted with a cheer from those onboard.

For the forty years, from 1871 to 1912, Pelorus Jack guided ships through those dangerous waters, saving thousands of lives.

During those years, only one ship struck the jagged rocks and sank. Why? In 1903 a drunken passenger shot at the porpoise, just nicking him. For two weeks the animal disappeared, and when it returned to work, it would not guide that one ship, which soon struck the rocks and was lost.

The drunken passenger thought his ship was safe, he didn't think he needed the porpoise. He didn't realise that they were doomed without its help. It was just the same with the disciples, when they got caught in a storm, on the Sea of Galilee.

Let us focus on a well known event in Jesus' life, recorded in the Gospel of Mark, Chapter 4: 35-41(NKJ)

> *35* On the same day, when evening had come, He said to them, "Let us cross over to the other side."
> *36* Now when they had left the multitude, they took Him along in the boat as He was. And other little boats were also with Him.
> *37* And a great windstorm arose, and the waves beat into the boat, so that it was already filling.
> *38* But He was in the stern, asleep on a pillow. And they awoke Him and said to Him, "Teacher, do You not care that we are perishing?"
> *39* Then He arose and rebuked the wind, and said to the sea, "Peace, be still!" And the wind ceased and there was a great calm.
> *40* But He said to them, "Why are you so fearful? How *is it* that you have no faith?"
> *41* And they feared exceedingly, and said to one another, "Who can this be, that even the wind and the sea obey Him!"

Imagine the scene, if you will. It had been a very eventful day, in the life of Jesus and his disciples. Jesus has spent another day with the crowds, taking them through some of his first parables, on the shore of the Sea of Galilee.

On this day, the eager multitudes press on Him so closely that He has to use Peter's boat as a pulpit, out on the lake, a little way from the shore. Day after day, Jesus had ministered to crowds of this size, scarcely pausing for food and rest, and constantly being harassed by the Pharisees. As the evening draws on, Christ craves seclusion that will allow Him relief from the pressure of the multitude, and time alone with His Father. So, at His direction, the disciples all got in the boat and hastily set sail for the other side. Yet, many of the crowd clamoured to be in the presence of Jesus. Greatly impressed by His teaching and His compassionate manner, they couldn't get enough of Him. So, they piled into other fishing boats lying near the shore, and followed. The Saviour, overcome with exhaustion, lay down in the stern of the boat and soon fell asleep.

The Sea of Galilee is really just a large lake, 21 km in length and 11 km broad. Therefore, it would seem that this short journey should be over in no time at all. On the other hand, the position of the lake, in the depths of the Jordan rift and surrounded by hills, renders it liable to atmospheric down draughts and sudden storms. So, when the disciples saw the clear sky quickly become overshadowed with dark clouds, experience told them that a storm was brewing. But they were not worried. You see, they were hardy fishermen and the lines on their weather beaten faces showed that they had been in many a storm, and had guided their craft to safety.

The wind swept wildly, down the mountain gorges along the eastern shore, whipping waves into the frenzy of a raging tempest. The mountainous waves began to rock the boat vigorously, pitching it to and fro, as if by the hands of mighty demons. They found that their quick thinking, strengths and skilful efforts at battling the storm were all to no avail. They sensed that this was no ordinary storm. The waves, lashed into fury by the power of the deafening winds, smashed fiercely against the boat, threatening to capsize it.

The experienced sailors concentrated and combined their efforts to steer the boat through the waves, keeping it upright, but all their efforts could not prevent the waves from dashing over the side of the boat. The situation was hopeless, and they were at the mercy of the elements, which beat upon them, from all sides. Already the boat was sinking. As water filled it, fear took its toll on each one of them; and you can imagine as their hope began to fade, all courage seemed to go with it. I can hear one of them saying, "Whose idea was this, anyway?" Another answers, "It was Jesus who wanted to sail across the lake." Then one question seems to appear on the face of every disciple. "But, wait a minute, where is Jesus?" Absorbed in their efforts to save themselves, they had forgotten that Jesus was on board. But now, seeing that they laboured in vain and only death faced them, they remembered at whose command they had set out to cross the sea. Jesus was their only hope. In their helplessness and despair they cried out, "Master, Master!" But as the wind blew, the sound reverberated in their faces.

They were unable to see Jesus, asleep in the stern of the boat, due to the dense blackness of the storm that hid Him from their sight. They stumbled around, calling and searching for Jesus. But, each time, the roaring of the tempest drowned their voices. Soon, it was apparent that the waters would swallow up their boat. Suddenly, a flash of lightening pierced the darkness and they saw Jesus lying asleep. He was undisturbed by the tumult. He was undisturbed by the deafening sound of the howling winds, undisturbed by the tossing waves, undisturbed by the roaring thunder, undisturbed by the enveloping dense blackness, undisturbed by the water filling the boat, and undisturbed by the fear that seizes the disciples in its vice-like grip. Jesus, asleep in His Father's care, lay undisturbed.

Wouldn't it be good if we could exhibit the same simple, child-like trust in the safety of our heavenly Father's love? But, the disciples couldn't understand it: Jesus sleeping like a baby in such a storm. They were astonished. And in their amazement and despair, they exclaimed, "Teacher, do you not care that we are perishing?" How could He rest so peacefully, while they were in such danger and were peering into the jaws of death? Jesus roused Himself; the flashes of lightening revealing a peace, that only heaven can bring, on his face. Jesus witnessed the look of terror on each man's face, and as the disciples grasped the oars to make one last effort, Jesus rose to His feet in the boat. Lightening flashed, illuminating the whole scene as the members of the crowd in the surrounding boats, which had been brought close together by the storm, looked on, in spectatorship.

As Jesus lifted His hand, all nature recognised it - the hand that gave sight to the blind; the hand that touched the lepers and made them clean; the hand that formed man, in the beginning. And in a calm, deliberate, commanding voice, Jesus told the storm to "Hush!" "Be still." And all who witnessed the scene were amazed, as the storm obeyed His will (Mark 4: 39).

The original Greek text suggests that the reaction was

instantaneous. As the words were uttered, the storm ceased, immediately, like the flipping of a switch. The storm ceased. The billows sank to rest. The clouds rolled away and the stars shone forth. The boat rests upon a quiet sea. Then Jesus turning to His disciples asks sorrowfully, "Why are you fearful?" "Don't you have any faith?" (Mark 4:40) You're with Jesus now. When I'm around, the deaf hear, the lame walk and the blind receive their sight. You're with Jesus now. Does that not count for anything?

The disciples and all those who saw the miracle, were greatly shocked. You see, they were expecting Jesus to pray. They woke Him, in desperation, that He might petition the throne of God for help. They were not expecting Him to stand up - He whom they spoke to and associated with, as we do with each other, He, Jesus, a man for all intents and purposes, encumbered with the weaknesses of humanity; they did not expect Him to stand up and merely tell the storm to 'cool it'. These are not the actions of a weak human, who is dependent on His Father's, God's, divine protection. But, to see the elements of sea and wind, which are no respecter of man or beast, to see nature recognise His voice and obey instantly, was staggering.

It could only mean that nature recognised the voice of its Creator. Nature recognised the voice of the One who, on the first day of current time, said, "Let there be light!" and there was light. Nature recognised the voice of the One who called the wind and the seas into existence. Nature recognised the voice of the Creator, and obeyed. A mixture of awe and dread seized the disciples as they murmured one to another, "Who can this be, that even the wind and the sea obey Him!" (Mark 4:41) And for many, who had not made up their minds about Jesus, that day was the turning point.

This miracle, and the events that led to it, serve as a great lesson for us today, as Christians. It is a warning against placing too much confidence in self and in our ability to save ourselves. You see, as long as we realise our hopelessness, and our total dependence on God, we are all right.

The disciples failed to guide their boat safely through the storm, because they trusted in their own efforts: they thought they were experienced sailors; they had seen it all before; they had guided many a boat safely through a storm. Well, big deal, they had never seen a storm like this. Let me tell you this, there is always a bigger, more terrifying storm around the corner. People, even Christians, trust themselves too much these days. We are too satisfied with our own efforts; we are always advertising how many baptisms we had, and seldom mention how many of the population out there that we have not reached. We go on about the countries we have reached and are having success in. What about right here in England, Britain? There are little more than 20,000 Seventh-day Adventists! How much is said about the rest of the population, the other 59,980,000? We are too trusting of ourselves and our efforts, just like the disciples. I can hear Jesus saying to the church of the Laodiceans, "Write to those Modern Christians, I know your works that you are neither cold nor hot; I wish that you were cold or hot. So then, because you are lukewarm, and neither cold nor hot, I will spit you out of My mouth. Because you say I am rich, and increased with goods, and have need of nothing, you do not know that you are wretched, and miserable, and poor, and blind and naked" (Revelation 3: 14-17).

Too often we forget how weak, wretched and miserable we are as human beings and how sinful we are, by nature. We forget that we are totally incapable of making the right decisions for our church; too often the name of the Chairman for the Committee of the Board of Directors for the church, is not Jesus. And I wonder if, like the disciples in the boat, in the storm, if something could be wrong with our picture. I wonder, could Jesus be sleeping in our churches?

Now, don't get me wrong. I'm not saying that your church hasn't got a connection with God. Far from it. Remember, there were lots of other boats, with other people in them, in the storm; but Jesus was physically in only one boat. Is Jesus in your boat, your church, today? Could it be that we leave Him to sleep, while we direct the church and our lives in ways that are our own? For too many Christians today, Jesus is nothing more than an 'at-your-convenience' pet, whom you feed with a bit of prayer in the morning and a little bit more prayer in the evening and take Him out for walks on weekends, just to keep Him happy. No, this is not the way to treat our Creator, Redeemer and Friend.

Too many of us have Jesus sleeping in our lives. Why? Because we forget that we are wretched, miserable, weak and sinful. We are becoming too self-sufficient. We trust ourselves so much that we have decided that we are saved and there is nothing that the devil or anybody else can do about it. How did we arrive at this state?

Paul was not so satisfied with himself, when he said, "I am carnal, sold under sin. I do not understand my own actions. For I do not do what I want, but I do the very thing I hate" (Romans 7:14, 15, NKV). He realised the misery of sin. "Oh wretched man that I am! Who shall deliver me from this body of death?" (Romans 7: 24, 25). I thank God, through Jesus Christ our Lord. We have no good reason to be self-satisfied, for without Him, we are nothing.

What is the focus of the story of Jesus sleeping in the boat?

In Mark 4: 35, Jesus says to them, “Let us pass over to the other side.” They were setting sail for the other side, under the instruction of Jesus. They were actually following His command. So, what went wrong? They were so absorbed in their own efforts to carry out His will that they forgot all about Him. That is what is happening to us today. Many times I’ve been so absorbed with carrying out His will and resisting temptation, as He wants us to, that very often all I can think about is the temptation. I forget all about Jesus and what He has to offer. I find that the times when I have kept my head and asked Jesus for the help I need to focus on Him, I usually lose sight of the temptation. If we forget about Jesus, the devil is more than likely to win every time.

We have to wake up to Jesus in our lives. We have got to let go of this self-sufficient “I’m alright, Jack!” attitude and say, “Lord, don’t you care that we perish?” (Mark 4:38). Until then, God’s hands are tied, and He is, figuratively, asleep. Even when we try to obey God, unless we ask for His help, unless we let Him live for us, we will fail. Because, I can tell you, it is not enough to obey God! You may be following His commands like the disciples on the boat, and still mess up like they did! Why? We find out in Matthew 7: 21-23:

> *21* Not everyone who says to Me, 'Lord, Lord,' shall enter the kingdom of heaven, but he who does the will of My Father in heaven.
> *22* Many will say to Me in that day, 'Lord, Lord, have we not prophesied in Your name, cast out demons in Your

name, and done many wonders in Your name?'
23 And then I will declare to them, 'I never knew you; depart from Me, you who practice lawlessness!'

You have to get to know God as your personal friend. You cannot treat Him as a stranger or a cash-point or a pet. You must strike up a one-to-one relationship with Him; not just be in the same boat as him! Not just using His name for our convenience, without relating personally to him.

So, what is the solution, how can we fight this self-sufficient attitude that pervades our boat and our lives?

The answer obviously is, God must be in control! Once you get that right, everything else falls into place. (see 2 Corinthians 5: 17; Galatians 2: 20 and Romans 6: 15, 16, 20-23). Do you get the idea of what Paul is talking about here? It is like John the Baptist, when he said, "He must increase and I must decrease" (John 3:30). That must be our attitude.

Don't pray for strength to carry on; pray for weakness (see 2 Corinthians 12:9,10) to hand over to Christ; pray for helplessness, to submit to Christ; pray for hopelessness, to make you rely on Christ. Jesus must direct your whole life - He must live it for you. Everything must be surrendered to Him, for His direction. It is not enough that you acknowledge that you are weak, you have to become weak; He must increase and I must decrease. You have to become like a child to enter the Kingdom of Heaven. Wasn't that what Jesus said? Only by becoming dependent on God, like a child, can God make you spiritually mature.

You will find that as you become weaker and less self-sufficient, your hold on God will get stronger and stronger. God will give you peace and you will realise that He is able to sanctify you, through weakness (2 Corinthians 12: 9), for He must increase and I must decrease - my self-sufficiency must decrease.

The words of a poem illustrate the need to replace self-sufficiency with total dependency on God:

As children bring their broken toys
With tears, for us to mend,
I brought my broken dreams to God,
Because He is my Friend.
But then instead of leaving Him
In peace to work alone,
I stayed around and tried to help,
Through ways that were my own.
At last I snatched them back and cried
"How can you be so slow?"
"My child," He said, "What could I do?"
"You never did let go."

We need to let go, today. We need to let go of the oars and let Christ steer our boat through the storms of life. Jesus says, "I am the first and the last." He came once to redeem us and He is coming a second time to reward us. We shall be caught up in the clouds to meet Him in the air, and so shall we ever be with the Lord! He died for us and He rose on the third day, and when He came triumphantly from the grave, He brought some of the captives of death with Him, as trophies of His victory over death. He says, "Behold I am alive forevermore, Amen; and have the keys of hell and of death!" (Revelation 1:18).

This is good news!

We know He is wonderful - the mystery of His plan of salvation is too wonderful even for angels to understand it. He is faithful and true. He died for you and me, but He is alive for evermore. Although the devil may continue to lead us to destruction, Jesus is gonna fix him! While we are in heaven, the devil is going to be here on earth, on his own, all by himself. You know what, I just can't wait! You see, as the branch is to the vine, I am His and He is mine. So, until then my heart will go on singing, until then, I will carry on, until the day my eyes behold that city, until that day I will carry on and on and on.

God sent His only Son to die for you and me - they crucified him on a tree. He stands and knocks at your door. You see, God is not dead No, He's alive! But God and sin they just don't mix. So, if you want to go to heaven give Him your life, before it is too late. He will fill you with His love divine. Through you, His love will draw your friends to Him! [change ending]

6

RAISE THE BATTLE CRY!

Psalm 47

Some weeks ago, I read a small news report in a local newspaper, entitled: "Air Ambulance Called to Fall."

It read: "Virgin's air ambulance landed on a tiny playing field in Carpender's Park on Friday afternoon to ferry an injured window cleaner to hospital. The helicopter had been called after Mr Malcolm Males suffered back injuries falling from a ladder in the Hoe. But it was decided Mr Males was not as seriously injured as first thought and he was taken to Watford General Hospital by ground ambulance. His condition is now described as comfortable."

The article continued to say that a small crowd had gathered around the helicopter, which was on stand-by in a nearby field, in order to take the window-cleaner to a specialist unit in Whitechapel, East London. When the crew realised they were not needed, the helicopter left the scene, creating huge gusts of wind from its blades. As I read this report, it occurred to me that the injured window-cleaner is like us, as Christians, when things go wrong.

We are ready to call on God for help and, twenty-four seven, God is there, on standby, just like the helicopter, waiting to rescue us from our problems. He is ready to apply His specialist care, specifically tailored to our problem. Sometimes we suddenly decide we do not need God, and instead, seek help from some human agent, whose plans for us turn out to be not as sophisticated as God's. Instead of being taken care of by the specialists in Whitechapel, the crème de la crème prepared by Divine providence, we choose to be taken on a bumpy ride in a ground ambulance, to the casualty units of the 'Watford General Hospitals' of human solutions, all because we thought we did not need heaven's help. Indeed, our condition is now described as 'comfortable.' But at times, all confidence in human ability and mortal efficacy fades away, as God allows a real crisis to flatten our man-made walls of self-sufficiency and 'convenience Christianity.' It is at times like these that crises can make or break our faith.

God allows trouble to disrupt our worlds, with two purposes in mind - to drive the wanderer back into His arms and/or to encourage and strengthen faith. The question is, How should the Christian respond to crisis? The answer, of course, is to be found within the pages of time - a time that was and is yet to come. The Bible is a book that was written long ago; it transcends time. The word of God is addressed to both ancient and modern man.

In the story, in 2 Chronicles 20, we are told of a king of Judah, Jehoshaphat, who finds himself in a crisis. But firstly, what sort of man was he? The Bible tells us in chapter 17,'...the Lord was with Jehoshaphat, because he walked in the first ways of his father, David.' This is quite a compliment. It would seem Jehoshaphat was trying to emulate all that was good about David, who was declared to be 'a man after God's own heart.' Jehoshaphat 'sought the Lord God of his father,' the Bible says, 'and walked in His commandments, and not after the doings of Israel.'

As you can see, the Bible speaks highly of Jehoshaphat. What did he do when the crisis stakes were raised against him?

The story, in chapter 20, tells us that 'the children of Ammon, and with them others besides the Ammonites, came against Jehoshaphat to battle.' News reached Jehoshaphat that a great multitude of soldiers, of several armies, was coming against him. The Bible says, Jehoshaphat was afraid - a natural human response to the threat of crisis. Jehoshaphat feared the situation, but he feared God more; and to fear God is to recognise that He is bigger than any situation you may find yourself in. The Bible says, 'And Jehoshaphat feared and set himself to seek the Lord and proclaimed a fast throughout all Judah. And Judah gathered themselves together, to ask help of the Lord: even out of all the cities of Judah they came to seek the Lord' (verses 3,4).

Remember the question: How should the Christian respond to crisis?

Jehoshaphat's first response was the correct one. The help of all heaven is just a whisper, a single thought pattern away. God can pick up the vibes of His children. How else could He answer prayers before they have even been said? And so it was that Jehoshaphat looked to God when trouble found him. And like Jehoshaphat, we must recognize that one man's crisis is the church's crisis. Not only the person experiencing the crisis should pray, but the whole congregation should unite in prayer.

The Bible concurs, 'All Judah came together to ask help of the Lord.' And although books have been written and many sermons preached on the subject of prayer, we still do not appreciate, nor understand its power. A crisis comes to drive us to our knees, and we pray, not to empower God to act on our behalf, but to unite our will to God's will and to be united with each other in one accord.

On the day of Pentecost, in the upper room, the followers of Christ were assembled together praying, emptying themselves of all self-will; praying for each other and praying that God would empower them to do His will. They were united in prayer and purpose - they were all of one accord in one place, hearts and minds were united as one in purpose. And at that moment, anything could have been accomplished. Because their hearts were fully surrendered to God's will, God was able to pour out His Spirit in a way that had never been done before.

When people are united, and they pray, things happen! "All Judah gathered together and all the cities of Judah came to seek the Lord. Jehoshaphat stood in the congregation of Judah and Jerusalem, in the house of the Lord, before the new court, and said, O Lord God of our fathers, aren't You God, in heaven? And don't You rule over all the kingdoms of the heathen? In Your hand, is there not power and might, so that none is able to withstand Thee? Aren't You our God, who drove out the inhabitants of this land before Your people Israel, and gave it to the seed of Abraham, Your forever friend? And they lived there, and built You a sanctuary therein, for Your name, saying, if, when evil comes upon us, the sword, judgement or pestilence, or famine, we stand before this house, and in Your presence, (for Your name is in this house) and cry unto You in our affliction, then You will hear and help."

Do you see what is happening here? Can you understand what Jehoshaphat is saying? Basically, he is saying, "You are God, and there is nothing too hard for you." Prayer is an expression of faith. It is simply a vote of confidence in everything that God does. It is an acknowledgement of the way in which God has helped, in the past, and it is recognising that God is able to rescue us from whatever predicament we find ourselves in. Jehoshaphat, after building the confidence of those around him, through his prayer, gets to his specific request: "And now, behold, the children of Ammon and Moab and mount Seir, whom You would not let Israel invade, when they came out of the land of Egypt, but they turned from them, and did not destroy them. Behold, I say, how they reward us, to come to cast us out of Your possession, which You have given us to inherit. O our God, will You not judge them? For we have no might against this great company that come against us; neither do we know what to do; but our eyes are upon You" (2 Chronicles 20:10-12).

Notice how Jehoshaphat ends his prayer. He does not say, "For we have no might against this company. So, if you could just triple our number, we would be able to handle things." He does not say, "Lord, we have no might against this great company against us. So, if you could just help us build a superior weapon of mass destruction, we will take it from there." No! He says, "We have no might against this great company that come against us, and neither do we know what to do." That is important. Yet he continues to say, "But our eyes are upon You, God," not "upon ourselves." In other words, we are watching to see what You can do for us.

All men of Judah stood before the Lord, with their wives and their children, expectantly waiting to see what God would do. You know, we are told we should pray without ceasing, but so often we pray to God as if He is deaf. When frequently, all that is needed is for us to stand still and see the salvation of the Lord. But we drone on and on praying in 'earnest', but not quite believing that our request may be granted - quite like the company of followers that prayed for Peter's release from prison and then did not believe he was standing at the door. We sometimes pray and are surprised when God answers; but whether God takes a long time to answer or He answers instantaneously, He always answers.

Yes! When God's people pray, things happen! God Himself answers! This ordinary man, Jehoshaphat, spoke and he said, "Hearken you, all Judah and the inhabitants of Jerusalem and you king Jehoshaphat, so says the Lord to you. Be not afraid nor dismayed by reason of this great multitude; for the battle is not yours, but God's." Sometimes God cannot give us any answer other than, "Be still and know that I am God," because we cannot see the bigger picture, as He does. We may not know the reason why He does what He does, but God works in mysterious ways and we should not question His methods. As far as God's plan is concerned, we tend to function on a 'need-to-know basis.' Yet so often we do not need to know. "I am that I am," God said to Moses (Exodus 3:14).

The eternal struggle with the devil to thwart God's plan, cannot be ended, nor God's will accomplished by human might nor human power, but "by My Spirit, says the Lord of Hosts" (Zechariah 4:6). Ephesians 6:12 tells us, "… we wrestle not against flesh and blood, but against principalities, against powers, against the rulers of the darkness of this world, against spiritual wickedness in high places." And so, God will tell us at times, "Be not afraid, nor dismayed for the battle is not yours, but God's." The Judeans were told to go down against their enemy. God said, "You shall not need to fight this battle; set yourselves, stand still and see the salvation of the Lord with you…" (2 Chronicles 20:17)

Remember the question we are asking ourselves: How should the

Christian respond to crisis? We have seen, so far, that in the midst of the crisis, Jehoshaphat set himself the responsibility to seek the Lord. We have seen how the congregation was called together and that a fast was proclaimed. We have seen how all Judah came together to ask the Lord for help. And how every man, woman, child and suckling babe stood before the Lord, awaiting His reply. We have also seen that the Lord answered promptly, telling them to stand still and see His salvation. To get a clearer answer to the question, how should the Christian respond to crisis, lets look in the book of Acts.

In Acts 16:13, 25, 26, we pick up the story of Paul and Silas, who had been publicly beaten and falsely imprisoned without a trial. "And when they had beaten them, they cast them into prison, charging the jailor to keep them safely. Paul and Silas were thrust into the inner prison, and their feet were fastened in the stocks... At midnight Paul and Silas prayed, and sang praises unto God; and the prisoners heard them. And suddenly there was a great earthquake, so that the foundations of the prison were shaken; and immediately all the doors were opened, and every one's bands were loosed."

There they are, Paul and Silas, devout men of God. A false charge has been trumped up against them as a result of them restoring a slave girl, who had an evil spirit, which took away the business earnings of a couple of slave owners. Their backs have been beaten until they were raw – several layers of skin have been ripped off with cruel whips. Their feet have been placed in the stocks, putting them in an extremely painful position. Their first response is to pray, and, to our credit, many of us might have done the same. But how many of us would feel like singing happy songs of praise to God? It seemed to all, who heard them, that they were happy to be in the predicament in which they found themselves. The Bible says, they sang! They sang praises to God; they sang song after song, after song of praise and thanksgiving.

Is that what Jesus meant, when he said, "Blessed are you, when men shall revile you, and persecute you, and shall say all manner of evil against you falsely, for my sake. Rejoice, and be exceedingly glad; for great is your reward in heaven?" (Matthew 5:11,12). Yes. That is why Paul and Silas could sing, and we, as Christians, should be no different. We should sing and rejoice when crises come our way, because it means that God has chosen us to be with Him in glory.

So, there they were, at midnight, singing in prison, with blood still dripping from their backs. Then suddenly, the Bible says, "...there was a great earthquake, so that the foundations of the prison were shaken: and immediately all the doors were opened, and every one's hands were loosed." Things don't only happen when God's people pray: things happen when they sing, as well. So, how should the Christian respond to a crisis? Is it simply enough to pray?

Paul and Silas did not think so. The early Christians who were thrown to the lions or burnt at the stake did not think so. David, who wrote and sang psalms and danced before the Lord as he brought the Ark of the Covenant back to the city of Zion, did not think so. The children of Israel, who marched round the walls of Jericho seven times on the seventh day, and brought down the walls with a thunderous shout of praise, did not think so. Gideon and his three hundred men did not think so and Jehoshaphat certainly did not think so either.

It is not always enough to pray in response to a crisis. There is power in our noise. We, as modern Christians, often fail to realise this. We overlook it in our quest to unite our will with God's and be one with each other in our struggle against adversity. The first verse of Psalm 47 says, "O clap your hands all you people, shout unto God with the voice of triumph!" There is power in our noise! Why then, are we afraid to clap in our worship services?

Don't you know that when we sing, the angels join in and the devil's ears ring. As we praise God, the angel chorus is raised and the devil is dazed. Our claps are like slaps and when we shout the devil runs out. There is power in our noise! And when our noise is praise and thanksgiving to God - things happen!

Walls fall down, earthquakes rock the foundations and prison doors fling open, shackles are loosed and battles are won without arms, as enemies flee from the advancing ranks of the people of God. Yet, prisoners of sin listen and jailers of God's people and their whole families give their hearts to Christ and are baptised.

2 Chronicles 20:18, 19, 21-23 says,

> "And Jehoshaphat bowed his head with his face to the ground: and all Judah and the inhabitants of Jerusalem fell before the Lord, worshipping the Lord. And the Levites, of the children of the Kohathites, and of the children of the Korhites, stood up to praise the Lord God of Israel with a loud voice on high. And when Jehoshaphat had consulted with the people, he appointed singers unto the Lord, and that should praise the beauty of holiness, as they went out before the army, and to say, 'Praise the Lord; for His mercy endureth for ever.' And when they began to sing and to praise, the Lord set ambushments against the children of Ammon, Moab and mount Seir,

> which were come against Judah, and they were smitten. For the children of Ammon and Moab stood up against the inhabitants of mount Seir, utterly to slay and destroy them; and when they had made end of the inhabitants of Seir, every one helped to destroy another."

In other words, God caused all the armies that came against Judah to destroy each other. "And …Judah …looked unto the multitude and behold they were dead bodies fallen to the earth and none escaped" (verse 24). There is power in our praise!

Jehoshaphat had not been instructed to make his army into a choir. Yet, we see in verse 22, that it was when they began to sing and give praise that God began to act on their behalf. God had said, "Ye shall not need to fight in this battle"(verse 17), and so the army went out armed with nothing. No Judean swords were raised, no Judean spears were hurled, no Judean bowstrings hummed and no Judean arrows were released. All Judah stood still and saw the salvation of the Lord.

Praise is the battle cry of the Christian warrior. The battle cry was effectively used by soldiers, who often sang in unison on the battlefield. It was an identifying hallmark, which filled them with bravery that seemed to dull the pain of wounds and put a little bit of extra energy into a soldier's sword arm, as he would rain down blows in a concerted effort to break his enemy's resistance.

The battle cry was also prized for its ability to strike terror into the hearts of the enemy, who were known to drop their weapons and run like rabbits from the ferocity of a ruthless sounding army. In the same way, praise, the battle cry of the Christian warrior, unites us with our Leader and Saviour, Jesus Christ, as we attack adversity on the battlefield of life! Praise is our identifying hallmark. It marks us out as Christians, followers of our Lord Jesus Christ, which fills us with courage. It dulls the pain of crises and gives us a glimpse of our God and an extra edge as He makes the joy of our praise rain down upon our archenemy, the accuser, striking terror to his heart!

Satan hates it when we praise God. He knows that praising God makes us happy because, he, himself, remembers how he used to feel when he used to sing and shout praises to God, and those were simply the happiest times of his life. But it is too late for him. He has cheated himself out of everlasting happiness. He has made his bed and now he must lie on it. But misery loves company. Satan doesn't want to lie on his bed alone. The worst thing you can do to Satan, is to lift your spirits and erase all negativity from your mind by singing praises to God. The noise we make gives him a headache and makes him long for the days when he used to lead the choirs in heaven.

So raise the battle cry of praise, when you are able, and sing. Sing when in triumph, sing when in trouble, sing when in peace, sing when in panic, sing in the morning and sing at midnight. Sing, and keep on singing. Sing like the Christians who sang while lions were attacking, while flames were burning them at the stake. Sing like the Africans in slavery, who were told by their Christian masters that it was God's will that they should be enslaved, but they sang on in spite of the whip. They praised God no matter what, and that was the secret of their strength that inspired fear in their masters. We too must learn the power of the battle cry. Praise God when you are in trouble. Praise God when things appear dark. Praise God when it seems your prayers are not reaching beyond the ceiling. Praise God even when you don't feel like it, because God is bigger than your situation.

Are you a slave to sin? A hypocrite, a double agent that brings a mask of external righteousness to church and discards it during the week? Sound your battle cry! God is greater than your sin! Are you in debt up to your neck? Is the bank about to foreclose on your house? Sound the battle cry! God is bigger than the bank. Have you messed up your studies? Are they about to kick you out? Sound the battle cry! God is greater than the Academic Standards Committee! Are you sick and tired of being sick and tired? Sound the battle cry, God is bigger than your illness! Are you bereft of a loved one and losing the will to live? Are you useless in all you do? Sound your battle cry! The Word says, "He gives power to the faint and to them that have no might "(Isaiah 40:29). God is greater than your grief!

Praising God helps strengthen our belief and our confidence in Him. Isaiah 26:3 says of God, "You wilt keep him in perfect peace, whose mind is stayed on You; because he trusts in You." So, if praise keeps our mind on God, which, in turn, inspires us to trust Him. Then:

Sound the battle cry
See the foe is nigh,
Raise the standard high for the Lord.
Gird your armour on
Stand firm every one
Rest your cause upon His holy word.

Strong to meet the foe
Marching as we go
While our cause we know
Must prevail.
Gleaming in the light
Shield and banner bright

Battling for the right
We ne'er can fail.

Rouse then, soldiers!
Rally round the banner!
Ready, steady pass the word along
Onward, forward, shout a loud hosanna!
Christ is Captain of the mighty throng!

So now, you tell me, how should the Christian respond to a crisis?

7

GIANT KILLER

1 Samuel 17:38-40; 44-47

The date is May 26. The year is 1982. A Japanese fisherman is busy tying up his boat, when, all of a sudden, he looks down as he feels the boat descending quickly; just as it would feel when someone presses the 'down' button in an elevator. Looking overboard, he notices the water receding rapidly and starting to rise as it does so. Realising exactly what this meant, he knew he must flee the boat in search of higher ground, before he found himself face to face with a powerful, giant wave, destroying all in its path.

As he ran, he noticed a group of school children having a picnic on the beach. There was no time to warn them before the tidal wave hit. They were totally unprepared and they were all washed out to sea. As soon as the wave receded, the fisherman found his boat and went to rescue the children. He was able to rescue ten, as others clung to floating wood and offshore rocks. But thirteen of the forty-three children drowned. There had been an earthquake about fifty miles away, and within two minutes from the time of the quake, the seismic wave hit the beach where the children were picnicking. They had no warning or idea that they would face death in the form of a 30-foot giant wave.

But whether unsuspecting or not, we all have our giants to face in this life. Challenges and obstacles in our path, that, at times, threaten to sweep over us like a seismic wave, and wash away all that we hold as dear. And so, we are afraid, and, like that fisherman, all we want to do is to turn tail and run for cover. But running will not stop that wave from hitting and doing its damage. In life the giant must be faced and the challenge met. But there are times when men's hearts fail within for fear of the giants they face, when forces we have no control over seem to conspire against us, to work our destruction.

Are you facing a giant of a problem today? Is there some huge mountain that stands in your way? Is there a tidal wave of a challenge that threatens to sweep away everything you have ever worked for? Well, I have good news for you! We serve a mighty God and He is able to transform you into a giant-killer!

What is a giant-killer? Well, it's a term that is often used by newspaper reporters, especially in sports, where a team of no reputation succeeds in beating the team most favoured to win. For example, when Bolton Football Club beat Manchester United in 1958 , the papers were heard to say, "Giant Killers!"

When Jamaica, a country that is without snow, found itself with a bobsled team in the 1988 Winter Olympics - competing against countries like Norway and Switzerland, for whom bobsledding is a major sporting event - and when Jamaica got their football team into the World Cup in 1996, people might have been heard to say, "Giant killers!"

Whenever a person or a group of people get together and accomplish what formerly would have seemed impossible, it seems as if our minds are cast back to that famous tale, of a mere youth, of a boy called David, who killed a ten-foot giant named Goliath! But what many forget about this tale is that it was not merely a boy who faced Goliath that day, but the resources of God!

The whole army of Israel listened to the challenge of the giant and not one man was found within that army who was willing to go and face him. There was not one man in that army whom God could use to meet the one who had defied Him. So God called David from his sheep. Yes, it was no accident that David was there! Only a man after God's own heart can defeat a giant! God chose David because he fully trusted in Him. David had a child-like quality in his trust and total dependency on God, which could not be found in any other man.

It was this child-like trust in God that prompted David to write in the Psalm 121:1, "I will lift up mine eyes unto the hills, from whence cometh my help. My help cometh from the Lord, which made heaven and earth." It was this child-like trust in God that prompted David to write in Psalm 27:1, "The Lord is my light and my salvation, whom shall I fear? The Lord is the strength of my life; of whom shall I be afraid?" David's trust in God was complete and he knew that his God was bigger than any giant!

The writer is thinking of people like David, when he declares in Proverbs 28:1, "The righteous are bold as a lion." The Bible tells us, in 1 Samuel 17:38, that Saul armed David with his armour, put a bronze helmet on David's head and also armed him with a coat of mail (1 Samuel 17:38). Is this what happens when we do not trust God? Because we cannot see the Almighty, we often feel we cannot be sure that He is out there, somewhere, protecting us.

So what do we do? We look for physical means of protection. Saul tried to give David the benefit of his human protection, but as Christians and like David, we have the resources of God and we must not seek human means to face the giants that Satan sends against us!

The Bible says, in 1 Samuel 17: 39, that David fastened Saul's sword to his armour and he tried to go, but he could not because he was not used to them. So he took them off. David wanted to make use of God's resources! Physically, he was a boy, but spiritually, in his relationship to God, he was a baby. Spiritually, a Christian reaches full maturity in his or her relationship with God, when they become a helpless babe in God's arms!

David was totally dependent on God. Saul's weapons of human solutions were totally unsuitable to him. "And David said to Saul, I cannot go in these, for I have not tested them". If we are to be the champions of God, if He is to make giant killers of us, we must not test the unreliable, insecure armour of human design. We must not get used to settling for human solutions to our problems, because with God there is always a better way. We cannot always see His design, but God sees the bigger picture and His resources are always best.

And so David took off the king's armour and went out to the Philistine as he was. "And he took his staff in his hand, and chose him five smooth stones out of the brook, and put them in a shepherd's bag, which he had, even in a scrip; and his sling was in his hand; and he drew near to the Philistine" (verse 40).

It must have seemed cruel to send a small, inexperienced youth, such as David was, against this great giant of a warrior. Yet, no one murmured against the folly of the king in sending a shepherd boy to his death, for fear of being chosen to take his place. As for the king, he was already regretting how easily he was taken in by the boy's courageous words. Seeing him, now picking his way toward the giant, armed with nothing more than a sling and a few stones, Saul wondered if he should turn away, so that he would not be sickened by the inevitable, terrifying sight of the giant making short work of the boy.

But what neither Saul, nor his men realised was that David was armed to the teeth, with God's resources. It seemed to them that he was walking out against this giant, unprotected. What they could not see was the armour that he *was* wearing: an invisible armour, tailor-made, to fit much more snugly and to offer protection far beyond that of King Saul's. This armour was indestructible and designed to assist rather than hinder whoever may wear it.

David was wearing the armour that Paul speaks of in Ephesians 6:17. David was facing his enemy fully clad in the armour of God. The Bible says, "He chose five smooth stones from the brook, and his sling was in his hand." The first stone had him girding his loins with truth. He chose a second stone, buckling on him the breastplate of righteousness. As he chose the third stone, his feet were shod with the preparation of the gospel of peace. His fourth stone was his shield of faith. And the fifth stone crowned him with the helmet of salvation. And his sling was in his hand, the sword of the spirit, which is the word of God, sharper and more penetrating than any two-edged sword.

David was armed to the teeth with the resources of God as he stood before Goliath that day. When the Philistine looked about him and saw David, about 17 years old, he scorned him.

I used to think, along with other folks, that Lennox Lewis could not be much of a fighter because he looks too good! It seems the bigger and uglier you are, the more people will respect you as a fighter. So Goliath scorned David because he was small, youthful and good-looking. And so it was that the more Goliath looked at him, the more he felt insulted; the more he despised the army of Israel and its king for presuming to waste his time, sending a boy, so clearly unskilled in the art of single combat.

"This dwarf of a boy had obviously never seen a battle before, let alone fought in one! And if that wasn't bad enough, they didn't even bother to fit the boy with some decent [armour]. Instead, he comes out to me with a stick, as if he's coming merely to beat a dog. This boy will pay dearly for their insolence. So they think I'm a pushover, do they? Sending this boy to me wearing no armour and armed with only a stick?

"Come here, boy! I'll feed you to the birds of the air and to the beasts of the field!" But what Goliath failed to realise was that he was not facing a boy, nor was he facing a man. Goliath was facing the God of all heaven and His resources on earth.

David warned him, "You come to me with a sword, and with a spear, and with a shield: but I come to you in the name of the Lord of hosts, the God of the armies of Israel, whom you have defied. This day will the Lord deliver you into my hand; and I will smite you, and take your head from you; and I will give the carcasses of the champion of the Philistines this day to the fowls of the air, and to the wild beasts of the earth, that all the earth may know that there is a *God* in Israel. And all this assembly shall know that the Lord saves not with sword and spear; for the battle is the Lord's, and He will give you into our hands" (verse 45-47).

When we, as Christians, are called upon to face giants on the battlefield of life, it is to prove to the heathen, to the atheist, to the fool who the psalmist declares, "…has said in his heart that there is no God" (Psalm 14:1), that there is a God, and that just as we believe in a brain that we cannot see within our heads, we believe in the God that made heaven and earth; the God, who is out there, and looks down on us; the God who can be personal to each one of us, because He sent His own son, who gave His life as a ransom for all.

Often the greatest challenge and the biggest giant that we face in this life, is learning to let go of our lives and let our Redeemer and Friend direct us in the way we should live. The battle against the giant of self is a daily one. But if you allow Jesus to conquer yourself, there is no giant that can come up against you and win. We must remember that the battle is not ours, but the Lord's.

And so it was, that the giant rushed towards David. David reached within his shepherd's bag, selected the stone that was the shield of faith; placed it into the sling, in his hand, the word of God, which is the sword of the Spirit. He wielded it slowly at first, getting faster and faster. When he let fly the stone, God guided it. The Lord was fighting the battle; the stone found its mark. When we allow God to battle on our behalf, we can never fail. And as the giant rocked on his feet, and then began his long fall to the ground, David stood still and saw the salvation of the Lord. And with the giant's own sword, David cut off his head. What the giant took to be his strength, turned out to be his weakness. The weapons of human uncertainty turned out to be his undoing.

The lesson for us in this famous tale is that God is bigger than any and all of the giant challenges that we must face in this life. And if we would only recognise this, we would remember to face these giants, fully clad in the armour of God. We will know not to test human solutions, but to use God's resources every time.

So what giant do you face today? Are you in debt up to your neck, struggling to meet the payments of that mortgage or that overdraft? Is your finance beyond human management? Seek Jesus! He is the greatest financial consultant! My God is the Creator and Owner of all things; there is nothing too hard for Him (Jeremiah 32:17).

What giant do you face in your life today? Is it the giant of human relationships? Maybe it is your mother-in-law you cannot get on with. Maybe it is a close family member you have fallen out with. Maybe your marriage is on the rocks and your unbelieving spouse just cannot share your joy in Jesus! Our God is a God of love and He can teach you how to love; all love comes from Him and no human can truly love without Him!

What giant do you face today? To the student who studies, He is a great Teacher! To the sick, He is a Great Physician and if it is not His will to take your illness away, He can help you cope! He will give you the grace to be a giant-killer!

Jesus says, "My grace is sufficient for you, for My strength is made perfect in weakness" (2 Corinthians 12:9) Do not put your trust in human solutions to giant problems. Look to God! The foolishness of God is wiser than man's wisdom, and the weakness of God is stronger than man's strength.

We need to get to know Jesus better, so that when we are offered human alternatives, we can say with David that we "cannot go with these because we have not proved them." Only the tried and tested solutions of God, though sometimes unorthodox, constitute a perfect fit. We need to know Jesus to the point that His ways are all we are used to, as was the case with David.

So who is this Jesus? Do you know Him? Abraham knew Him as a Shield and his exceeding great Reward (Genesis 15:1); Balaam knew Him as the voice of his donkey (Numbers 22:30); David knew Him as his Shepherd (Psalm 23:1) Daniel knew Him as the stone cut out without hands that smote the image and became a mountain that filled the whole earth (Daniel 2:35); Elijah knew Him as the still small voice (1 Kings 19:12).

Who is this Jesus? Do you know Him? Gideon knew Him as the Angel of the Lord, the Stranger who called him a mighty man of valour (Judges 6:12); Hosea knew Him as the Husband, whose people Israel, were like his rebellious and unfaithful wife (Hosea 4:12-14); Isaiah knew him as the One who is "brought as a lamb to the slaughter" (Isaiah 53:7); as the One in whom "there is no beauty or majesty" (Isaiah 53:2); as the One who is "despised and rejected of men; a man of sorrows and acquainted with grief" (Isaiah 53:3); the One who surely "has borne our grief and carried our sorrows" (Isaiah 53:4); as the One who was "wounded for our transgressions"; as the One who was bruised for our iniquities, and with His stripes we are healed" (Isaiah 53:5); as the One who "hath poured His soul unto death and was numbered with the transgressors, bearing the sin of many and who made intercession for the transgressors" (Isaiah 53:12).

Who is this Jesus? Do you know Him? Joshua knew Him as the Captain of the Lord's host (Joshua 5:15)! Jacob knew Him as the ladder, that staircase that reaches ever upward to the very gates of heaven (Genesis 28:12). Timothy knew Him as the only means of reconciliation, the only medium of communication between God and man (1 Timothy 2:5)!

Who is this Jesus? Do you know Him? John the Evangelist and beloved disciple of our Lord, knew Him as the light that shines in the darkness (John 1:5). John the Baptist knew Him as the Lamb of God who takes away the sin of the world (John 1:29). Jude knew Him as the One who is able to keep you from falling and to present you without fault before the presence of His glory, with unspeakable joy in exultation (Jude 24). Moses knew Him as the Lord, the Lord God, merciful and gracious, longsuffering, and abundant in goodness and truth (Exodus 34:6).

Who is this Jesus? I'll tell you who this Jesus is! He is the One, who knew no sin, that we might be made the righteousness of God in Him (2 Corinthians 5:21). He is the One who was treated as we deserve, that we might be treated as He deserves. He was condemned for our sin in which He had no share, that we might be justified by His righteousness, in which we had no share. He suffered the death that was ours, that we might receive the life which was His (E G White, *Desire of Ages, p25*).

I can tell you, He is the One who "made Himself of no reputation, and took upon Himself the form of a servant and was made in the likeness of men" (Philippians 2:7). He is the One, who being found in fashion as a man, humbled Himself and became obedient unto death, even the death of the cross (Philippians 2:8). He did this so that we, who have been redeemed may now declare with one voice, "there is a fountain filled with blood, drawn from Emmanuel's veins, and sinners plunge beneath that flood lose all their guilty stains!"

Who is this Jesus! Do you want to know Him? It is He, who has said, "Come unto me all ye that labour and are heavy laden and I will give you rest." It is He, who says, "Take my yoke upon you and learn of Me, for I am weak and lowly in heart," and He promises today that "you shall find rest unto your souls," For He says, "My yoke is easy and My burden is light" (Matt 11:28-30).

This same Jesus is able to make you a giant-killer. It is He who, for the joy that was set before, endured the cross, disregarding the shame and is now sitting at the right hand of God (Hebrews 12: 2). He says to you today, "Behold, I come quickly and My reward is with me..." (Revelation 21:12) and "to him that overcome, will I grant to sit with Me in My throne" (Revelation 3:21).

Do you want to be a giant killer today? Open the door to your heart and let Jesus into your life. God says, " I have loved you with an everlasting love" (Jeremiah 31:3). He loves you! He loves you so much that He knows everything about you! Don't you know it is God from whom we borrow each breath! And as one preacher puts it, "He is awfully kind to put breath in your body so you can spit in His face." He knows you – He even knows the number of hairs on your head (Luke 12:7). God said to Jeremiah, "Before I formed you in the womb, I knew you; before you were born I set you apart." (Jeremiah 1:5) He says the same thing to you today! He knows you better than you know yourself. Don't you want to know Him too?

God has never turned His back on anyone who has really known Him and come to love Him. God has never failed anyone.

Open your heart to Him today, and when you come to know and love Him, you will be able to declare, with the songwriter,

'Tis so sweet to trust in Jesus
Just to take Him at His word.
Just to rest upon His promise
Just to know, "Thus saith, the Lord"

You will say:

> I’m so glad I learned to trust Him,
> Precious Jesus, Saviour, Friend
> And I know that you are with Me
> And will be with me till the end.
>
> Jesus, Jesus, how I trust Him
> How I proved Him o'er and o'er!
> Jesus, Jesus, precious Jesus
> O, for grace to trust Him more.

8

KEEPING IT REAL

Isaiah 29:8-13

It was a warm summer's day, not unlike any other day in Jamaica. The sun was shining with sufficient potency to give anyone's complexion a treat. And being near the sea, the wind, which had exhausted itself in the Atlantic and slowed down considerably over the Caribbean Sea, was now blowing gently inland. It was positively refreshing. Or, to put it another way, "Bwoy de breeze was sweet!"

My family and I were holidaying in the great JA. We had driven from Clarendon that morning, to visit Negril. It was now time to return and my brother was at the wheel with my dad beside him in the passenger seat. My mother had just sat down on the back seat. While my brother and my dad were heatedly debating some subject or other, I opened the rear door on the passenger side and was preparing to climb in. Suddenly, to my astonishment, the car sped off, with the door still ajar, leaving me standing outside on the road with my leg still raised, poised for entry. The car was gone and was now lost to my view. I waited and waited for it to return, and as time went on it became clear to me that they had left me behind and did not even know it! A full twenty minutes passed before I saw the car again and when I asked my mother whether she had noticed my absence, she said, "Oh, I was so upset!" Apparently, my dad and brother, who had left me without realising it, could not understand a word in five of what she was saying. So, they ignored her.

We do that don't we? We are so caught up in the humdrum events of our lives that we speed ahead, in our own human strength and we leave Jesus behind; or, we may rush out of the house and say a quick prayer, when we remember to, and hurry on to wherever we are going. But sometimes, even when we set aside time for Jesus during our devotional prayer and Bible study, we drive off and leave Jesus with an astonished look on His face and one leg still raised, poised for entry. We enter and leave our closet without the powerful presence of the Holy Spirit, who will help us to understand and correctly interpret God's instructions for our personal lives, and in our devotional Bible study, we leave Jesus behind and do not even know it!

At the time of the prophecy recorded in Isaiah 29:8-13, which was directed to the inhabitants of Judah and, particularly, Jerusalem, the people had left God and yet, did not seem to know it. So intent were they on ignoring God's messengers that they could not comprehend how far, as a nation, they had sunk into wickedness. They did not realize that by ignoring God's laws and ignoring His messengers, they were ignoring God Himself.

Jerusalem was the city that held the temple of God. Judeans and Israelites from all over Palestine used to journey there to worship God. But now, in their decadence, they burned incense to idols of silver, gold, wood and stone in God's holy city. They severed themselves from God. They bloodied their hands with the lives of their own innocent children, burning them with fire in sacrifice to Baal. Yet, the people believed themselves to be righteous. God said in Isaiah 65:5 that He had never known a people "holier than thou!" Yet, the smoke of their iniquities burned in His nostrils. God sent messengers to warn them, but these they mocked, scorned, threw into prison, tortured and even sawed in half. God is longsuffering, but He is not unfeeling. Time and time again, feeling compassion for the weakness of the human condition, God offered pardon if they would turn from their sins. But they would not take him seriously. When God sent Jonah to tell the Assyrians of Nineveh of their impending doom, a whole city of heathen people, who devised methods of torture that would make the medieval Spanish Inquisition look like a Sunday stroll in the park, repented. People who knew nothing of God, from the greatest to the least, put on sackcloth and sat in ashes, and neither man nor beast tasted food or water in that city, but all cried mightily to God. They knew nothing of God, yet they took Him seriously. But God's own people, who knew all the stories of deliverance, did not believe Him. His own people would not listen. Finally, God sent a messenger, by the name of Jeremiah. Chapter 19:3 says, "Hear the word of the Lord, O kings of Judah and inhabitants of Jerusalem. Thus says the Lord of hosts, the God of Israel, behold, I will bring evil upon this place, which whosoever hears, his ears shall tingle." But what did they do? Pashur, a false prophet, who was the son of a priest and chief governor in the house of the Lord, stepped up to Jeremiah and struck him in the face. Then, they put Jeremiah in the stocks.

The message God sent was, "I can see you are all sleeping, but you will wake up and you will find that your souls are empty and your existence meaningless, because you've been sleeping all along." In verse 8, God illustrates the sleep of ignorance and self-deception. He says, "It shall even be as when a hungry man dreams, and, behold he eats; but when awake his soul is empty: or as when a thirsty man dreams and behold he drinks, but when he is awake, behold he is faint, and his soul has appetite." Or as the New King James Version puts it, "...his soul still craves."

What is He talking about? The sleep of ignorance, verse 10, "For the Lord hath poured out upon you the spirit of deep sleep, and hath closed your eyes..." Look around you today and see the spirit of deep sleep among us, around us, and inside of us. That is the situation we find ourselves in today. We are *all* sleeping! I am not referring to your forty winks, your afternoon siestas, or even your basic eight hours sleep. The situation that we are considering here, is the sleep of the unconscious. What is it that characterizes every unconscious sleeping person? Two things, (1) they are blissfully unaware of what is going on in the real world; (2) they are conscious only of what is taking place inside themselves, in the world of dreams.

Both these characteristics of the unconscious sleeper are consequential of the other – you cannot separate the two. But what do they mean to the sleeping person if s/he is oblivious to what goes on in the real world? In basic terms, it means that the five senses on which s/he

depends are non-functional. Therefore, if someone decides to steal your car, you will not see them, though it is under your very window. And neither will you hear them, because being asleep, you are oblivious to what is going on in the real world.
If a fire rages in your house, you will be cooked in your beds if no one wakes you - poisoned by the smoke you did not smell, and burnt by the fire you did not feel. This is all because your five senses are non-functional – you're oblivious to what is going on in the real world. In the inner world of the unconscious, the world of dreams, three things are usually true:

Firstly, the dreamer is the hero, the good guy up against the baddies. Even if you kill someone in your dream, you are doing what is the heroic thing to do. There is no right or wrong about it, because you are the hero. You can do no wrong.

Secondly, the unconscious sleeping person has no concept of time. There is absolute timelessness. As regards to the passing of time, someone once said to me that they closed their eyes at 3pm on a Friday to get a little rest before choir practice, but when he opened them again it was 11pm. There is no concept of time or the passing of time, during sleep.

Thirdly, the unconscious sleeping person went to sleep trusting their senses. That is to say, very often one believes that what one sees, hears, smells, tastes and touches is all real. It is this particular habit of the dreamer that our text speaks about. A sleeping person can eat or drink in a dream, enjoy the sight, smell and flavour of whatever they are eating or drinking, but will be acutely disappointed when they awake to find that it was not for real.

What does all of this mean? It means that we cannot see the truth clearly, from the illusion of all the lies that the devil seeks to deceive us with. Paul says, "For now we see through a glass, darkly…" (1 Corinthians 13:12). Many things are kept from us now and we who sleep will not see them until we are fully awakened and, so, we are unwary victims and, without Jesus, sometimes we are caught in the devil's trap, senseless, unable to hear the truth, because we are too busy listening to lies.

And so a girl listens to a boy who tells her he loves her. But nine months later she is alone. She was senseless. She thought it was love, so she could not smell the rat. She was senseless, so she could not feel the coolness of non-commitment and uncertainty in his caresses. Senseless, so she could not taste the bitterness of disappointment on his lips as they kissed. Senseless, so she could not hear the insincerity in his voice. Senseless, so she could not see the lust in his eyes. She was dreaming and so she sold her youth down the river for three little words that, for many, have no meaning at all. Just a password that gets the required "access allowed" to flash up on the screen. She was dreaming and thought she was eating, but when she awoke her soul was empty and her hunger remained. Dreaming, and got caught with society's standards - it's ok, everyone is doing it! The enemy feeds us his lies and we willingly eat and drink. We are willing ourselves into the heavily drugged sleep of self-deception, shackling ourselves to the pathetic miseries of this world and thinking that is what life is all about. And we leave Jesus behind, forgetting that all we see is temporal, but that the things unseen are eternal, as if, like the people of the world, we did not know it.

You see, sex will never be able to replace love, and money cannot buy you joy. Nor will popularity give you peace, and the best pleasures this world has to offer can never take the place of Jesus. Jesus said, "I am come that they might have life, and that they might have it more abundantly" (John 10:10). We are all sleeping.

That is why men and women of the world can wonder around in ignorance, working beside so-called Christians, sharing buses with them, going to school alongside them and living next door to them. These Christians, fully clad in the whole armour of God, are senselessly oblivious to what goes on around them. While they are dreaming, men and women of the world ignorantly aspire, as do some of their Christian counterparts, to the 'life of Riley' – to the best that life can offer. They believe that that is what life is all about. They think that they are eating and drinking and do not realise that one day they will wake up, when they look into the eyes of Jesus, the Creator of the universe, when every knee bows and every tongue confesses Jesus Christ is Lord. Then they will say, "You mean to tell me, that stuff about evolution and natural selection was just a load of rubbish, made up by misguided scientists? You mean to tell me that existentialism and pantheism and atheism and atheistic pantheism are also rubbish? You mean to tell me that these writers did not hear the voice of God from heaven say? " "Who is this that darkens My counsel with words, without knowledge?" (Job 38:2). "How could I have known?"

As they look a little longer at the compassionate face of Jesus, the personification of love, they will realise how empty and meaningless their life has been without Him. They will realise, too late, that He was what they wanted all along and did not know it. They would do anything for Him now, but the time for that has passed. It is too late. The soul is empty, but the hunger remains.

Some of us, who have accepted Christ, have not woken up to the realisation of how empty and meaningless our existence is, without Him. Some of us, who have accepted Christ have not realised that we ourselves are leading empty and meaningless lives, trying to make it on cheap grace without Christ or the power of the Holy Spirit. We do not seem to know that we have left Jesus behind and we are trying to exist without Him. We are living in a dream world – fast asleep! Senseless!

We do not see a homeless person on the street. Senseless! We do not hear a cry for help from someone in trouble. Senseless! We cannot smell the filth of the evil one. Nor can we feel the damage we dish out to others through our careless, and at times, deliberate remarks. Senseless! We are fast asleep, unaware of what we are experiencing, living in a dream world of our own, in which everything and everyone is exactly what they appear to be. We are always the hero, "I can do no wrong because I'm the good guy up against the baddies. Therefore

Sister so-and-so is wrong, and I am right. Pastor so-and-so is wrong and I am right. Brother so-and-so is mistaken and he should listen to me. Elder so-and-so is foolish – this is how it should be! I'm always the hero." And so, we have left Jesus behind, and being in a sleep, we have lost all sense of time and reality. We do not seem to realise that we are living in the time of the end, and that Jesus will come soon. There is no time for bickering and backstabbing. No time for contention and conflict, no time for hearsay and idle talk. No time for squabbling and scandal mongering. No time for tightness and triteness. No time for meanness and money cheating. No time for farcical fakers and fractious faultfinders. No time for criticizing and cutting down our fellow brothers and sisters. There is simply no time!

Now is the time to be getting ourselves right with God and allowing the Holy Spirit to transform us and prepare us for the latter rain, the power of God's Holy Spirit, shared among ordinary lay people who will finish the work. But we are not ready! We hunger and thirst after righteousness, but we will not be filled. We enjoy our church experience and we are not afraid to get involved. We have done voluntary work, distributed religious literature, read poems, prayed prayers, sung songs, preached sermons; we have gone to every Bible study, ran to every specialist Bible Seminar, went to every evangelistic meeting, seen every Net link-up, been to every revival. We have made scores of resolutions and gone up for every appeal. Yet the soul is empty and the hunger remains, we are faint with the frustration and our souls still crave something. Why? It is because we have been dreaming, dreaming that we are eating and drinking; but if we will only wake up, we would realise that our souls are empty, hunger and thirst remains, and the soul still craves food. It is because we have been chewing on the cheapness of vaporous good intentions, we have been munching on the non-motivational skills of a catchy chorus. We have been tucking in to the triviality of temporary temperance and we have been feeding on the fleeting flimsiness of pseudo-sentiment and emotional highs. Then we have washed it all down with a worthless draught of wistfulness.

But now is not the time to feed on the empty, bland, artificially flavoured nothingness of emotive, churchy-brand entertainment. Now is the time to feed on Christ. If we do not feed on Christ now, while we have the chance, if we do not continually pray for the transforming power of His Holy Spirit and see Him work His miracles on our characters, we will end up just like the five foolish virgins.

This parable speaks to us about the time of trouble that we have yet to experience. Five were prepared and five were not. The text says that all ten virgins, both wise and foolish, fell asleep. Therefore, all ten had grown comfortable and, I believe, that speaks directly to our time. Nevertheless, all ten were letting their lights shine, being witnesses and doing God's work. The difference was that the five wise virgins had a real Christian experience, well nourished by the Holy Spirit, to fall back on; and the five foolish virgins had nothing.

Let's take a look at what the time of trouble means for us. The time we are living in now is feeding time, in which we allow God to take away our sinful natures and replace it more and more, day by day with the nature of Christ. One day God will be so confident of the job that He has done on His saints (and that does not include everyone who professes to be His followers) that He will step back in confidence and say to Satan, "I'm so confident of My children's faithfulness, I'm so confident of My children's love that I know that you may be able to attack their bodies, disfigure them, but you cannot touch their souls!"

The Bible says the devil knows his time is short. We think we know about time, but our three-score-and-ten-years-plus-grace-years, is like a flash to the devil, who has existed for thousands of years and knows the nature of man like the back of his hand. He is going to realise that his time has all but run out. You are talking about the full force of the powers of darkness descending with a vengeance, in the rage of those who know they have nothing to live for, meeting out havoc and annihilation and leaving carnage and desolation in their wake, as never before.

The protective and restraining power of a merciful God will appear to have been withdrawn from the earth. We will be left, apparently defenceless, against legions of demons who specialize in attacking the mind, attempting to erase and eradicate all Godly influence. Our only defence will be the knowledge of the scriptures, the memory gems we have learned. Do you think you have what it takes to remain true, when the Bible says he, Satan, will deceive, if it were possible, the very elect? (Matthew 24:24). Back then, when he was inexperienced, Satan deceived a third of the angels of heaven, who had been in the presence of God. Do you think you are ready to cope with his attacks?

Let us take a good, long and hard look at ourselves. We are all in Slumberland now, but some of us will wake up in time for the final outpouring of the Holy Spirit. The rest of us may not wake up until the time of trouble hits us and, by then, it will be too late. Those of us who have nothing to take us through the time of trouble are those who the inspired writings tell us, are crying, "peace and safety." We lull our hearts into false security and we dream, but not of danger. Then the cry goes out at midnight that the final crisis is upon us and our true characters are revealed. We see the sunken state of our Christianity. We perceive our pitiable and pathetic plight. We recognize our regrettable wretchedness. We discern our deplorable destitution and we beg others to supply that which we lack. But in spiritual things, no man can make up for another's deficiency. And if we have not co-operated with God, letting Him replace our old natures with a new one; if we have been content with a superficial work which does not go beyond enjoying church and having a regard for the truth, we will not know God.

We will not have studied His character; we will not have yielded ourselves to Him. We will not have held communication with Him. We will not know how to trust Him, or how to look and live; and therefore, our service to God will have degenerated into a form. We will be like those Ezekiel spoke about: "...they come unto thee as the people cometh, and they sit before thee as my people, and they hear Thy words, but they will not do them: for with their mouth they shew much love, but their heart goes after their covetousness" (Ezekiel 33:31). We have been too content to play church and treat Christianity as a game of 'Let's pretend'. Although we may sound convincing when we sing, "In a little while we're going home," all we can think of in our hearts is, "I want a man. I want a woman. I want letters after my name. I want more money. I want a better job. I want a nicer car. I want a bigger house. I want…!" So, God now looks at us and declares, "Forasmuch as this people draw near Me with their mouth and with their lips do honour Me, but have removed their heart from Me, and their fear toward Me is taught by the precept of men" (Isaiah 29:13).

It is not enough to hear the words of songs sung by people with beautiful voices, nor sermons by powerful preachers, nor to study doctrine, nor learn the memory verses. The church experience will not make you a Christian. What is needed is a real closet experience. What is a closet experience? Look up Matthew 6:6, where Jesus tell us we should not pray to be seen in church or on the street corners to look good, but we should enter into our private closets, where our heavenly Father can meet us in secret, and our Father who sees us in secret will reward us openly.

It is a kind of rendevous. 'Rendevous' is French for 'meeting', but in the English language is popularly used to signify the secret meetings of lovers. I cannot think of a better way to describe the closet experience. I have called this chapter, 'Keeping It Real' because the closet experience has to be kept real. It must not degenerate into a once-a-week, randomly selected encounter, timed according to whim exercise, nor must it become a daily recital of the usual prayer-like prose. It must be kept real. That means meeting with God on purpose, like a rendezvous, at a time you set the day before. It should be something you learn to look forward to, not another thing to get done. It has to be kept real. In order to keep it real, it must always be Spirit-filled. For without the Spirit of God, knowledge of His word is of no avail. Without the influence of the Holy Spirit on these daily or nightly meetings, repetitive prayer and reading of the Bible will not change your life. However, that is not to say that the reading of God's word is not vital to the work of the Holy Spirit on and in our lives. This could be one of those chicken and egg situations.

We cannot go up to our individual closet, shut the door, sit down and say, “Okay God, change me!” and then drum our fingers expectantly on the windowsill. No. The effort on our part comes in feeding on Christ, through His word. In the sixth chapter of John, Jesus says, “Whoever eats My flesh and drinks my blood, has eternal life…” (verse 54, NIV). “It is the spirit which gives life, the flesh counts for nothing… the words that I speak to you are spirit, and they are life” (verse 63).

Here we read and understand that it is not the literal flesh or blood of Jesus’ body that is being referred to. Nor is it the symbolic flesh and blood - the Bread and the Wine that we take in our communion services. No! Jesus said, “…the flesh counts for nothing….” It is the Holy Spirit that transforms the life, using the word of God, quick and powerful and sharper than any two edged sword! Growth in the Christian comes by the Holy Spirit and through the word of God that we are to eat and drink daily, for without them, spiritual life ceases and eternal life is lost. If we would obtain the abundant life Jesus speaks of, at the hand of the Holy Spirit, we must eat and drink, absorb and digest His words, not the ethereal emptiness of pipe dreams.

There is a rich source of scriptural food in the Bible: "Therefore shall you place these my words in your heart and bind them in your soul and bind them for a sign upon your hand and bind them on your foreheads.” (Deuteronomy 11:18). “And he humbled you, causing you to hunger, and fed you with bread, which neither you nor your fathers did not know; so that you might know that man shall not live by bread only, but by every word that comes out of the mouth of the Lord” (Deuteronomy 8:3). Psalm 119:9 asks the question, “How shall a young man cleanse his way?” "Your word have I hid in my heart that I might not sin against you" (Psalm 119:11). “Your word is a lamp unto my feet and a light to my path” (Psalm 119:105). "I have esteemed the words of his mouth *more* than my necessary food” (Job 23:12). "O you

dry bones, hear the word of the Lord" (Ezekiel 37:4). "Man shall not live by bread alone but by every word that proceeds from the mouth of God" (Matthew 4:4). "Heaven and earth shall pass away but my words shall not pass away" (Mark 13:31). "For whoever shall be ashamed of me and my words, of him shall the Son of man be ashamed, when He shall come in His own glory, and in His Father's, and of the holy angels (Luke 9:26)." "If a man love me, he will keep my words" (John 14:23). "And he that sat upon the throne said, Behold I make things new. And he said unto me, write: for these words are true and faithful."(Revelation 21:5). "Then Simon Peter answered, Lord to whom shall we go? You have the words of eternal life" (John 6:68).
Yes, indeed, Jesus has the words of eternal life, and keeping it real is that simple. If you want to maintain a real Christian experience, then go to your 'closet' each day, pray for the Holy Spirit and read, absorb and dig into the words of Jesus, and then let the Holy Spirit apply them to your life. *That* is keeping it real!

9

GET A LIFE!

2 Chronicles 25:1-11

1 Amaziah was twenty-five years old when he began to reign, and he reigned twenty-nine years in Jerusalem. His mother's name was Jehoaddan of Jerusalem.
2 He did what was right in the sight of the LORD, yet not with a true heart.
3 As soon as the royal power was firmly in his hand he killed his servants who had murdered his father the king.
4 But he did not put their children to death, according to what is written in the law, in the book of Moses, where the LORD commanded, "The parents shall not be put to death for the children, or the children be put to death for the parents; but all shall be put to death for their own sins."
5 Amaziah assembled the people of Judah, and set them by ancestral houses under commanders of the thousands and of the hundreds for all Judah and Benjamin. He mustered those twenty years old and upward, and found that they were three hundred thousand picked troops fit for war, able to handle spear and shield.
6 He also hired one hundred thousand mighty warriors from Israel for one hundred talents of silver.
7 But a man of God came to him and said, "O king, do not let the army of Israel go with you, for the LORD is not with Israel-- all these Ephraimites.
8 Rather, go by yourself and act; be strong in battle, or God will fling you down before the enemy; for God has power to help or to overthrow."
9 Amaziah said to the man of God, "But what shall we do about the hundred talents that I have given to the army of Israel?" The man of God answered, "The LORD is able to give you much

> more than this."
> *10* Then Amaziah discharged the army that had come to him from Ephraim, letting them go home again. But they became very angry with Judah, and returned home in fierce anger.
> *11* Amaziah took courage, and led out his people; he went to the Valley of Salt, and struck down ten thousand men of Seir.

It was the wedding of the century and the world was invited. We all looked on in anticipation as the world's most famous couple exchanged vows on the morning of the 29th July 1981, in St Paul's Cathedral. The soothsayers and well-wishers predicted calm seas and good times ahead.

Prince Charles and Lady Diana Spencer were, it seemed, perfectly suited. And our hearts were touched by their seeming example to us, of the beauty and innocence of young love. It was as if the childhood dreams of all, had come true, for two. It seemed to have all the makings of a perfect fairytale, where all involved in the fantasy live happily ever after. Yet, within five years, we found the two living separate lives, while faking togetherness for the cameras. Eleven years down the road and 2 children later, on the 9th December 1992, the royal couple separated. Then, in February of 1996, they announced divorce proceedings. What went so terribly wrong?

In their separate interviews and in the biographies that were written, Prince Charles' half-hearted approach towards the marriage came out as one of the causes of its failure. And Charles himself admitted that his heart was never in it.

Today, we find people adopting the same half-hearted attitude or approach towards living the Christian life. Mark you, they seem to be doing all the right things. They come to church every week;

they may even pay their tithe and give generous offerings regularly; they are very vocal on church issues; and you will find them to be faithful participants in church services and activities. Outwardly, there appears to be an adequate display of devotion to the church, faking, as it were, togetherness with God for the cameras. Yet, God knows when a person's heart is not in it.

Amaziah was one such person. He did all the right things, but his heart was never in it. The Bible says that Amaziah did that which was right in the sight of the Lord, but not with a perfect heart (2 Corinthians 25:2). Matthew 5:48 tells us, "Be perfect even as your father in heaven which is perfect". That is a tall order! Here the Bible seems to be asking us to do that which is not possible for us to do, that is to say, be like God!

Yet, only God can be like God! So, is there not some mistake here? What else did Jesus say about being perfect?

Jesus was praying to his Father in the presence of his disciples, who were hearing every word, and he said "I in them and them in me, that they [his disciples] may be made perfect in one" (John 17:23) . Aha! So it is possible to be perfect! We certainly cannot do it under our own steam; we are helpless to do the will of God with a perfect heart, without Christ in our lives. Only Jesus can create in me a clean heart and renew the right spirit within me! Only God in a person can make that person godly, in the truest sense of the word.

"I in them and you in me, that they may be made perfect in one". What Jesus is talking about here is the church. This prayer and blessing was the first step in the formation of the church. But, as we look at the adventures of the early church and then examine our own church of today, it becomes abundantly clear that they had something that we do not have.

What was it that made the difference in those earlier times? I hear you say that the Holy Spirit was very active in those times. Yes, indeed, He was. Yet, does not the promise of the Comforter belong to us, also? The Holy Spirit still ministers to us, here on earth. In fact, it is He that should be Director of the church, as He was in Paul's day. So, what makes the difference? Acts 2:1 says, "When the day of Pentecost was fully come, they were all of one accord in one place". What makes the difference? They were of one accord. Their spirit-filled lives were united into a church with a common goal – that of serving God whole-heartedly, with all their might.

But, what of our church today? We are like the church of the Laodiceans, talked of in Revelation: we are neither cold nor hot, we are lukewarm Christians (Revelation 3: 16). God hates our indifference. God hates our half-heartedness. God despises our abominable attitude of convenience Christianity. We come to church each week and we often leave unchanged. We are so caught up in our own lives that church just becomes part of our weekly schedule; just another component of the cycle, like the 'home-to-work, work-to-home, dinner, TV and bed' ritual that we endure each day.

Some of us grudgingly give our tithes and offerings, when we remember or can afford it, because the Lord understands. And prayer meetings? Well, we seem to have forgotten the meaning of the phrase. Not that many people appear to need it anymore. What has happened to the church? The church is not a building in which you worship. The church should be a community of the followers of Christ. There used to be a time when church members would spend nearly all their time together, realising that the church that prays together, stays together and grows together in Christ. What has happened to the church? One preacher said there used to be a time when people would come to church early and go home late. Now, we come to church late and want to go home early. Our zeal for spiritual things is all but gone. It would seem that, like Amaziah, we are doing that which is right in the sight of the Lord, but not with a perfect heart. Why? Because we, as a church, are not all with one accord. We are lukewarm!

We are lukewarm because, we, the members of the church, are too busy faking togetherness with God for the cameras! No one wants to be continually reminded that he is a worthless, no good sinner! When God makes us conscious of His words and we see ourselves truly in His looking glass, we feel too unworthy to approach Him. You know its true! We are sinful and we therefore feel that we cannot pray! We forget the words of Isaiah 53, that

> He was wounded for our transgressions, he was bruised for our iniquities; the chastisement of our peace was upon him; and with his stripes we are healed. All we like sheep have gone astray; we have turned everyone to his own way, but the Lord hath laid on him the iniquity of us all!

We need not feel unworthy, because, as the hymn says, "Jesus paid it all, all to him I owe, sin had left a crimson stain…", but oh "…He washed it white as snow." But, because we fear the shame, we decide that we would rather continue hurting than experience the healing of repentance. Rather like the person who would prefer to endure a toothache, than go to visit the dentist.

The resulting complication of all this, however, is that when we become complacent and apathetic in spiritual things, and we get used to serving God half-heartedly; we learn not to expect much from God. Since we are not saintly in character, we do not expect great and astonishing miracles and clear indications of God's leading in our lives, to be a frequent occurrence! This was no different with Amaziah. He had paid just over a ton (1000lbs) in weight of silver for some fighting men - that is about $200,000 or around £140,000 sterling.

Amaziah invested a great deal in these mercenaries. But God did not want Amaziah to rely on himself and men who did not trust in Him. God wanted, instead, to show Amaziah that He could supply all his needs. A man of God, a prophet with no name, came to Amaziah saying "O king, let not the army of Israel go with you, for the Lord is not with Israel". But you see, Amaziah had already paid for the men. Amaziah did not consult God and did not put his trust in Him. So, he did not expect God to do anything wonderful for him.

What did Amaziah put his trust in? In creatures and in money instead of the Creator and owner of all things! We do that sometimes, don't we? We allow bank managers and credit merchants to tell us we are blacklisted and therefore worth very little, just because we are not wealthy and are constantly in debt.

We allow employers to tell us when we can go to church and when we must work. We allow the TV to dictate the quality of time we spend with our families. We allow professors and other academics, who do not know our God - who holds the future, to tell us we have no future! We continually put our trust in unspiritual things and ungodly people, who let us down over and over again, while our Almighty God is continually demonstrating His power in other people's lives!

Have you ever asked yourself why clear and astonishing indications of the providential workings of the Holy Spirit always seem to happen to other people and never to you? Why do these things always happen to others but not to me? I know the church. I have been there. You would think the most logical conclusion is that it is because my heart is not perfect, and this is why these things do not happen to me. It is a vicious circle!

Now, I am sure that Amaziah had learnt in church school how God parted the Red Sea for the children of Israel to cross. I am sure he had learnt how Israel marched around the walls of Jericho and how in response to their glorious shouting, the walls tumbled to the ground; he had learnt how God helped Gideon defeat the mighty army of the Midianites, with a mere 300 men; he had learnt about the legendary strength of Samson, and how, when filled with the Holy Spirit, he attacked the army of the Philistines, armed with nothing more than the jawbone of an ass, slaying a thousand men! Make no mistake about it, Amaziah had heard about the mighty deeds of his forebearers and he had seen the power of God manifested in others' lives. Yet, it may be that he just could not conceive God working such wonders in his own life - he did not put his trust fully in God.

Job had full confidence in God. Even though he was scarred by tragedy after tragedy, he was able to say of God, "Though he slay me, yet will I trust in Him!"

Like Jeremiah, Job liked to wallow in self-pity. Both of them cursed the day they were born, but they still had fire in their faith! Like Job, Jeremiah was a man who could not help but be devoted to his God. And because God was in his heart, it was his desire to serve God perfectly.

Many times Jeremiah said, "I will not make mention of Him, nor speak any more in His name. But His word was in mine heart as a burning fire shut up in my bones and I was weary with forbearing and I could not stay" (Jeremiah 20: 9). That is the kind of experience we want in our lives! I want to have fire in my faith so that it burns within me like a beacon. I want to be weary of holding my God in, and being helpless to watch as He spills out of my life to touch others.

But what is it that is stopping us from getting this fire? Why can't we seem to achieve Pentecost now? Is it because we have no fire, we are lukewarm and are content to stay that way? God says in Revelation 3:16, if you maintain your lukewarmness, "I will spit you out of my mouth". One day Jesus will declare an end to His ministry in the heavenly sanctuary. The Holy Spirit will be taken from the wicked as the door of probation is shut forever by God Himself. On that day, there will be no more intercession, and "he that is unjust will be unjust still, and he that is filthy let him be filthy still." That will be the pronouncement for those who have not allowed God to feed and sustain them His spirit.

And the prophet said to Amaziah, "O king, do not let the army of Israel go with you, for the LORD is not with Israel - all these Ephraimites. Rather, go by yourself and act; be strong in battle, or God will fling you down before the enemy; for God has power to help or to overthrow" (Verses 7, 8).

God gave him a choice. God never forces Himself on anyone, but He will let you know that His way is better - God's way never fails. Amaziah said to the man of God, "But what shall we do about the hundred talents that I have given to the army of Israel?" The man of God answered, "The LORD is able to give you much more than this." (Verse 9).

Amaziah has just spent about £140,000 on mercenaries, he has given the men a truck-load of silver, and the prophet says leave the men behind, because if you do not, you will lose. Of course, his first thought is for the empty coffers in his royal treasury. "Now, you tell me," Amaziah said, "what about the trailer-load of silver I've just handed over?" The prophet just stares at him as if he is stupid. "But man, the Lord is able to give you much more than this!"

God, our Father, is on our side. Jesus, our Lord and Saviour, came to this world and lived the perfect life that we could not and he died a hellish and violent death. He died for you, for me. He died for every misdemeanour, every offence and He died for every evil, iniquitous and deliberate, pre-meditated act. No person need be lost, the vilest person may wear Christ's robe of righteousness, washed in His blood. It is whiter than snow, and one size fits all! Jesus is on our side! The Comforter, the third member of the Godhead, who took over Jesus' ministry here on earth after Christ's ascension, and who is here with us today, is on our side. The heavenly host of angels, the messengers of God are all on our side! Why then do we allow things to come between God and us?

Jesus said, "I am come that they might have life and have it more abundantly" (John 10:10). So, get a life! Accept a life, because without God in us, we have no life. Jesus says, "Without me you can do nothing." Psalms 53:1 declares, "The fool says in his heart, there is no God." So much for the atheist! But for those of you who remain in the valley of decision, who feel deep down that you would like to know this Jesus who can make something beautiful out of your life, to you he says, "Be still and know that I am God" (Psalm 46: 10).

My question to you is, What do you need? Do you need a place to live? A soul-mate? A new car? The Lord is able to give you much more than these. What do you need? A spouse? A new job? A holiday? The Lord is able to give you much more than these too! What do you need? New friends, a family, money? Don't you know that the Lord is able to give you much more than these?! What do you need? Stability? Something to live for? God can provide all your needs according to his plan for you!

He can take you from the typical and the habitual; He can rescue you from the routine and the regular; He can call you from the customary and the commonplace; and He can do wonderful, astonishing things in your life, if only you will let Him.

Whatever you need, the Lord is able to give you much more! So, get a life, dear friend! Make God your supreme, number one. Then, in your life you will experience much elation, you will overcome your tribulation, and the devil can be brought under control.

Get a life!

Your sinful life will undergo disintegration, much to the devil's consternation; your heart will have fire like a great conflagration.

Get a life!

Others will see your consecration and want to make Jesus their aspiration.

Get a life!

You will be happy in God's exaltation. The devil will know only humiliation. You'll exceed everyone's expectations!

Get a life!

The Holy Spirit will be yours in the time of tribulation. Jesus will offer His congratulations.

Get a life, for God is able to do for you much more than you might think and although I cannot tell you what it is you need today, I know a man who can, and He is Jesus - the Man with the life-plan.

10

LORD, IF YOU HAD BEEN HERE...

On Saturday, 4th October, at around 7:55pm, I understood and felt how Mary and Martha felt at the death of Lazarus. "Lord, if You had been here, my brother would not have died." (John 11:20, 21).

That's how I felt, that evening, as I peered into my brother's unseeing eyes, calling his name and clapping my hands directly in front of his face, in some desperate effort to bring him back to consciousness. After all we had been through, how could he be dead?

The nurses gently stated that they would switch off the monitors now. When I asked why, my mother declared, "Because he's dead, son."

"No he's not!" I replied. "Do something! Do something! Somebody!" But clapping my hands and calling his name was to no avail. Earlier that day, I had preached at Stevenage Church, at their Youth Day of Fellowship. I mentioned in my sermon that my brother was in hospital, and that he was to graduate the following week with a 2:1 Honours Degree from Bristol University.

I did not know that my mother had called the church and spoken to my father, telling him that we were to come directly to the hospital. Then she searched for a specific pastor, whose presence Roger would not object to. When the pastor arrived with his elders, he explained to us what he was about to do. He said, "I will anoint Roger, but before we pray I will tell him that salvation is only a prayer away, and we will allow him to pray and make his peace with God." Then he said, "We have come to pray for the sick not the dying, we will be praying for Roger to make a full recovery." That's how he talked with us.

And when the prayer and anointing were finished, the pastor expressed that he had positive feelings about Roger making a full recovery. In fact, his expressions were such that, though I cried throughout the prayers, I dared hope that Roger would be restored to full health and things would once again be as there once were. If I were a different person, I would be very bitter with that pastor today. But, I talked with God, telling Him how He knew that Roger could serve Him better than I, and be a great soul winner for him, now that he had made things right and given his heart to Jesus. But there I was, 3 hours later, with my head on his stomach and my hand in his hand, the tears forming rivulets, as they dripped onto his cooling chest.

Oh God! Why?! Why did you allow this to happen? And that was the question, unspoken, in those sisters hearts when Mary also said, in words identical to her sister, Martha, "Lord if you had been here my brother would not have died."

The Bible says that when Jesus saw them all crying, he was moved and troubled. In the next verse, the shortest verse in the Bible, are those words, which say so little and yet so much. "Jesus wept" (John 11:35). Why did Jesus cry?

He cried for the human frailty of those of us who cling to this life with no hope of another. Running frantically and getting nowhere, like hamsters in a treadmill, clinging to all that is temporary: such as youth, beauty, and even life itself. If only He could show us the bigger picture – the wonders that He has in store for us: a place where beauty and innocence are common place; where there will be no more pain and no more death; where we will never grow old or have to be separated from those we love again. I believe that as the cold hand of desolation reached into my chest and closed about my heart, wringing tears from my soul, Jesus was crying. Crying for my grief and disappointment but crying that He could not show me the bigger picture of the life that awaits us all.

In times like these, it is hard to put aside grief and put your trust in God; when you feel you need to be angry at someone, it is hard to trust the One to whom you wish to apportion blame. And so, God is often the scapegoat.

I am amazed by the life of one man called Job, who, despite all that happened to him, refused to relax his grip on God. A man who declared of God, "I will trust Him even if He kills me." A man who, after losing all of his wealth and all ten of his children, who were killed in one day, said "The Lord giveth and the Lord taketh away. Blessed be the name of the Lord." (Job 1:21b) Now, those do not sound like the words of a suffering, grieving man. But Job suffered. And when his friends came to see him, after sitting with him for a whole week in silence, they accused him of bringing this disaster upon himself with some wrongful act. Job's friends saw disaster and tragedy as vengeful retaliations from God. But Job challenged them and questioned God to identify the cause of his suffering. But God did not answer in the way Job expected. His answer to Job's question was to show Job who God is.

You see, God is all we need to know. He is the solution to all of life's questions. He is the be-all and the end-all. The Bible calls

Him Alpha and Omega, the beginning and the end (Rev. 1:1). He is from everlasting to everlasting (Ps. 103:17). So, whenever we ask God a question or pray for something, in whichever form, His answer comes. His response will always be, "I am God."

God says, "I am not a man that I should lie, nor the son of man that I should change My mind. I am the Lord. I change not. As the heavens are higher than your ways and My thoughts than your thoughts. For My foolishness is wiser than man's wisdom and My weakness is stronger than man's strength." You can't question God. He is God!

My question was, "Why weren't you here? If you had been here my brother would not have died." But deep in my heart of hearts, I knew that God was there. He gave my brother the chance to talk with Him and make things right between him and his God. And I know that even if I do not make it, Roger will, one day, live once more and never see death again. What makes me so sure of this, is the story about the thief on the cross. Jesus was crucified between two thieves and you all know the story. One thief looked across at Jesus, as he hung there dying on that cross, and as he gazed into Jesus' face. He saw such peace and innocent beauty. In that face, he saw all that he ever wanted and did not know it. Deeper than that, he saw love, even for him. His own life flashed before his eyes: he saw himself stealing at a young age from other children at school; he saw himself creeping into people's houses at night; he saw himself in crowds, perhaps where Jesus himself stood, taking things from people's pockets, and his heart was broken!

And now, living on borrowed time, realising that all opportunities had passed him by, all his last chances had been used up, he felt too unworthy to beg for the forgiveness that he so desperately needed. But instead, he cried out, " Lord! Remember me! Lord! Remember me when you come into your kingdom." And Jesus answered and said, "I say to you this day, you will be with Me in paradise."

Like the thief, my brother chose the last moment to open up and surrender his heart to God. But I know that we all may not have that chance. One of us may be walking down the stairs tomorrow, and slip and break our neck, or have our life snuffed out in a car accident, like Diana and her lover.

No one can be sure of the length of his/her days. But, because we are young, we have no fear of death and so we live life on the edge. Like a baby who would crawl out of the top floor window of an 80ft building unless you stop it, we, also, fearing no danger, live our lives teetering on the brink of destruction. Always stepping over the safety line and existing just outside of God's principles of right living, like my brother, distancing yourself from all things to do with God. But thanks be to God, Roger was given the chance to make his peace with God, before he expired. Not all of us will be so lucky. But Roger now gives us all the chance to reconsider the paths of our lives that we have chosen.

We can continue to live in the fast lane, flirting with the jaws of death, or we can allow God, who created us and knows us so well that He has even numbered the hairs on our heads, to direct our lives. A man's heart may plan his way, but God directs his steps.

Mary said, "Lord if you had been there my brother would not have died." But I want to say, "Thank you, Lord, for being there, because if You were not there, my brother would not have the chance to live again."

APPENDIX ONE

FAR BEYOND THE CALL OF DUTY

by Dr Albert A C Waite and Catherine Anthony

On Wednesday, 16 August, over 600 people gathered in and around Stanborough Park church to pay their last respects to a young man, who, in life, had touched the lives of many, for good. They came mainly from the territories of North and South England but also from France, Germany and Spain. Among the group were over 30 pastors including Pastor C R Perry, BUC President and Pastor D W McFarlane, South England Conference President. They came to celebrate the life of Jeremy V Fletcher, who having returned from General Conference Session in Canada, preached his last sermon in Birmingham on Saturday 22 July, before going to Spain for a holiday, where he died suddenly on Saturday 29 July 2000.

As the procession of some twenty pastors lead by Stanborough Park's own R Vine took their places on the platform, one person whispered, "Was he a pastor?" As Dr Patrick Herbert, in whose church Jeremy preached his last sermon, stepped forward and with well selected words welcomed the crowd, informing them, briefly, of the impact Jeremy had had on the lives of people in his district; as Costa Vaggas announced and commented on, and we sang "When the Roll is Called up Yonder", it was hard to imagine anyone in attendance who did not want Jesus to come there and then! Pastor McFarlane in a combination prayer (words and music) gave one of the most touching and relevant public prayer we have ever heard, complemented by Alicia A C Waite playing Traumerei (Dreaming) a violin piece by Schumann. The crowd responded deeply with a 'Hmmm.'

Pastor Jude Jeanville, a close family friend gave the eulogy, in which he informed us that Jeremy Victor Fletcher was born on the 30th March 1971, the second son of Victor & Maisie Fletcher. Four months later, Pastor Watson Southcott dedicated him to the Lord at the Bedford SDA Church.

As a young child, Jeremy was fond of family worship. This daily event, with stimulating and exciting Bible stories, left an indelible impression on the mind of Jeremy. It no doubt influenced his future choices. His parents can remember vividly on one occasion during these special times when he unexpectedly said, "I wish Jesus would come now for me to look into his beautiful face".

When Jeremy was seven, the family moved from Stevenage to Watford. This enabled his parents to give both him and his brother, Roger, a Christian education at Stanborough Park School. At the age of 11, while attending Stanborough, Jeremy requested baptism and was baptised in the adjacent Park church.

After completing his secondary education, Jeremy registered for a BA degree in Theology, at Newbold College. Jeremy had sickle cell anaemia, but it never stopped him achieving his goals: in education, sports, extensive International travel and a full social life. As his father, Victor said, "Jeremy worked hard and play hard."

While at Newbold College, Jeremy participated in student organisation activities and contributed significantly to campus life. He was renowned for his oratory, acting and musical talents. Such was his flare for drama that many of his peers remember, with constrained laughter, his performances on British and International Nights at Newbold College. He graduated in June 1995, with a BA in Theology and he was awarded a commendation for going beyond the call of duty, and for courage and determination to get involved in campus life.

Jeremy was a tribute to his parents, who co-operated with God in giving both Roger (his brother) and him, the best that they could afford. Mr and Mrs Fletcher were parents who realised that they had to "train up a child in the way he should go", knowing that when he was older he and the training would not be separated.

Jeremy had a flare for languages. This lead him to study Spanish and Psychology at Middlesex University in London, which is affiliated with the University of Valencia, Spain. He spent one year in Spain, where he gained merit for his essay in Spanish. Jeremy was scheduled to teach Spanish part-time at Stanborough Secondary School in September 2000, while he completed the last semester at Middlesex for a second BA degree.

Victor said of his son, "Jeremy was my best buddy, as well as my son. He was my kung fu sparring partner into the evenings, which I always looked forward to. Jeremy shared his love and loyalty between his mother and I very effectively. He was a builder of human spirit. Whatever we asked him to do, he did it willingly. The death of Jeremy has left a void in our lives that can never be filled as long as life lasts. We didn't even get a chance to say goodbye to him."

No one can understand the love of a mother or the pain at losing a child so prematurely, except a mother. Maizie expressed this succinctly and with hope: "Jeremy was my best friend and confidante. As long as life lasts, he will be forever in my thoughts. Come, Lord Jesus, quickly come."

Jeremy's warm personality won him many friends, and admiration, right across the age spectrum. Here are samples of the tributes:

- Professor Michael Dreiscoll, Vice Chancellor, Middlesex University: "Jeremy was a very charming person, kind, gentle and humourous, who was very popular with staff and students alike.... He had made lots of friends among the people he met while in Spain and that he greatly enjoyed his time there.... It is difficult for me to say anything that will help you at this time, but if there is any way in which I or the university can assist, please do not hesitate to let me know."
- Greg Wilson, cousin and close friend: "I found him to be a man of God, a counsellor and a friend that loved at all times."
- Melanie Jeanville, aged 10: "God sent Jeremy for us all. He sent him to pick us up when we fall."
- Marisa Santos Vilaplana, Valencia, Spain: I met Jeremy at E. O.I. last year (1999) where I studied English and we often did homework together. We went to Madrid with my family. I'll always remember his sweet smile, his words about life, family and God and specially his courage to go on smiling when he was hospitalised.
- Juan Carlos Arocas (aged 17, Spain): "I will be seeing you brother, I'll be seeing you friend. It was an honour to have known you. Some day I will have the chance to do something big for you."
- Pastor Garry Gordon, college colleague and preacher at Jeremy's funeral said, "He was much more than just a personality, he had a passion for others and his constant, positive and sincere outlook, gave no place for negative thinking."
- Pastor Stefan Burton-Schnull: "What remains for me are memories of a lovely, loving, humorous, quietly bearing friend and brother."
- Dr Jeff Brown, former Senior lecturer, Newbold College: "Let

> the elements describe you: The wind would try to claim you, saying you influenced more people than you knew. The trees would try to claim you, saying your branches touched so many lives. The sun would try to claim you, saying you competed with it for the warmth you gave to people. Goodbye, my friend. Your death inspires us to live better - so we can see you again."

Jeremy lived the life of a Christian. His sudden death has left a void in the lives of those who knew him. His family and friends will mourn him for years to come. In the words of the well-known song, "I just looked around and he was gone." But as Dr Waite said in his tribute, "Although it is hard to accept the reality of today and the days ahead, we believe that soon, on the resurrection morning, Jeremy will have life again. Then his open grave will signal victory over death and sadness."

Jeremy was awarded his second BA degree from Middlesex University, which his parents collected in July 2001.

APPENDIX TWO

WHAT A TRIBUTE CAN NEVER SAY

by Olsen Roberts

A friendship is a special kind of relationship. It's the one type of relationship that provides you with an opportunity to get to know somebody outside of your immediate family circle and share something of yourself with a person who is not related to you. A friendship is a bridge that joins two people together, across a divide of unfamiliarity. And in the end, it is this ability to share and to care about someone, other than yourself, that true friendship is based upon. And true friendship will *always* attract the attention of others.

*****

A few moments in tribute can't begin to describe how Jeremy and I came to learn about the essence of true friendship, over a period spanning nearly 21 years. And a few words in tribute won't say something of how much value our parents placed on church life, so that our friendship stemmed and owes its existence directly due to our regular attendance of Sabbath School. And from that early beginning to this unexpected end, these few moments of tribute will not be able to illustrate how our friendship was always centred on our involvement in the church…

A few minutes in tribute can never portray how the length and extent of our friendship also owes itself to our ability and willingness to talk and to share. And if anyone knew anything about us at all, they would know that this tribute wouldn't be able to describe how much we certainly did like to talk and share:

From the times growing up where we used to argue about which one of us was going to become GC [General Conference] president and who would have to settle for the vice-president's role; to the occasions back in Sabbath School where Jeremy would attempt to relieve me of the mistaken belief that I had the greater Bible knowledge.

If only this tribute could demonstrate how Jeremy and I could always find something to share and how our parents were constantly at their wits end to know WHAT it was that we always found to talk about: Perhaps their concern came from the worry that the more we talked, the less anything else seemed to get accomplished; or perhaps it was the more understandable fear that the more and more we talked, the greater the danger they faced of becoming the primary source of revenue for British Telecom! And yet it was this incessant talking and sharing that built up an incredible awareness and understanding of each other that meant that no matter how long a period of time would elapse between speaking, as soon as we met up again, it was business as usual.

I wish that in these few moments this tribute could clearly illustrate how by the time of our 'teen years, not only was our friendship well cemented, but it was also well known. And how we had quickly got used to sharing in each other's experiences, and how it wasn't up until recently that we fully realised that the sharing of these experiences actually helped to shape the individuals we were. To the point where:

We mirrored each others mannerisms;

We carried much of each others characteristics;

We portrayed similarities in personality;

We sought the same sense of humour.

I would have liked this tribute to attempt to portray his infectious laughter and the unique type of laugh he had that demanded a person respond with a smile. And how, if our friendship ever had an unwritten rule, it would have stipulated that the pleasure that came from laughter was to be experienced regularly. And so, we would often reduce ourselves to tears over something we found amusing, despite the fact that the next person might be struggling to find the humour. Friendship with Jeremy taught me to laugh at myself and to do so often.

If this tribute could do such a friendship justice, it will come as no surprise to learn then, that Jeremy was the greatest influence a friend could be in my life. And this was exhibited in all manner of ways:
From advice about fashion, to ideas about music.
From advice about relationships, to ideas about studies.

But perhaps the greatest influence that came from the friendship was the joint and yet personal desire to work for God and to preach the gospel.

And, would that this tribute could plainly reveal a glimpse of what occurred to me just the other day: That the impact of Jeremy's life was all the impetus needed to bring people from all walks of life together, where nothing else seemingly would. And you need only take a good look around you to see for yourself the result of one life, and the impact it has made, bringing people together with people they seldom see and rarely know.

And to all those who too may feel impressed, and may wish to honour the life of my closest friend, and to all those who have yet to experience a friendship like the kind Jeremy and I have shared, I have a suggestion: Why not let this tribute also become a tribute to the one friendship that outlasts and runs deeper than all others; turn this tribute, dedicated to a friendship made on earth, into a tribute dedicated to a friendship with the God of Heaven and Earth. And like me, you'll come to realise that it is God that grants us the privilege of a relationship of a friend, in the hope that through such relationships with one another, we may in turn develop a closer relationship with Him.

******

"So now Jesus, friend to all God's children, be that friend to me.
Take my hand and ever keep me close to thee.
Never leave me nor forsake me, ever be this friend,
For I do need thee from life's dawning to its end."